# When Thinking Begins

*Lessons Learned From Helping
Preaverage Intelligence Individuals*

By

**ALBERT M. BARRETT, Ph.D.**
*Director of Psychology
Sunland Training Center
Gainesville, Florida*

CHARLES C THOMAS • PUBLISHER
*Springfield* • *Illinois* • *U.S.A.*

*Published and Distributed Throughout the World by*
CHARLES C THOMAS • PUBLISHER
Bannerstone House
301-327 East Lawrence Avenue, Springfield, Illinois, U.S.A.

This book is protected by copyright. No part of it
may be reproduced in any manner without written
permission from the publisher

© 1973, *by* CHARLES C. THOMAS • PUBLISHER
ISBN 0-398-02770-6
Library of Congress Catalog Card Number: 72-11607

*With* THOMAS BOOKS *careful attention is given to all details of manufacturing and design. It is the Publisher's desire to present books that are satisfactory as to their physical qualities and artistic possibilities and appropriate for their particular use.* THOMAS BOOKS *will be true to those laws of quality that assure a good name and good will.*

*Printed in the United States of America*
Q-1

| DATE DUE | | | |
|---|---|---|---|
| | | | |
| | | | |
| | | | |
| | | | |
| | | | |
| | | | |
| | | | |
| | | | |
| | | | |
| | | | |
| | | | |
| | | | |
| | | | |
| | | | |
| | | | |
| | | | |
| | | | |
| | | | |
| GAYLORD | | | PRINTED IN U.S.A. |

# WHEN THINKING BEGINS

*Lessons Learned From Helping
Preaverage Intelligence Individuals*

# FOREWORD

It is the purpose of this book to help awaken the mental power of those people who, through no fault of their own or their parents, have had to endure a burdensome struggle for existence. I hope these ideas help them in some way to gain a place in society's adventure in living.

*Albert M. Barrett, Ph.D.*

Gainesville, Florida

# PREFACE

It is not too often that a college professor actually sees his own *ivory tower* ideas come true in the tough world of practicality where it really counts. I have had this circumstance occur to me in the past ten years and it is most gratifying.

This book represents the culmination of classroom theory, research ideas and practical application converging together in a synopsis that I hope is helpful toward alleviating conditions for an unfortunate but blameless segment of humanity.

The methods and ideas were not wrought from unshatterable experimental proof but from the observant expedient hope that mostly they work.

The case histories are composites and hypothetical. They are representative of reactions observed in many preaverage intelligence people. These examples are composed of common elements seen in many different cases and allow generalizations that may be more meaningful than any single actual narrative.

I hope to change the semantics of *mental retardation* to *preaverage intelligence,* propose a workable theory, a manual of operations and a view toward the future that may improve the outlook of the more intelligent three quarters of society for that innocent lower quarter.

*Albert M. Barrett, Ph.D.*

528 N.W. 34th Drive
Gainesville, Florida

# CONTENTS

|  | Page |
|---|---|
| *Foreword* | v |
| *Preface* | vii |

*Chapter*

| | | |
|---|---|---|
| I. | INTRODUCTION | 3 |
| II. | THE IMPORTANCE OF INTELLIGENCE | 9 |
| III. | THE ABC KEY TO AROUSING OR ALERTING THE DORMANT POWER OF INTELLIGENCE | 15 |
| IV. | THE ABC ONE VARIABLE APPROACH | 32 |
| V. | THE IMPORTANCE OF THE BARRETT ABC METHOD OF DIRECTIONS IN SETTING THE STAGE FOR LEARNING | 36 |
| VI. | THE VALUE OF THE JIGSAW PUZZLE IN ITS DEVELOPMENT OF PREAVERAGE INTELLIGENCE INDIVIDUALS | 38 |
| VII. | A TOTAL STIMULATION ENVIRONMENT FOR PREAVERAGE INTELLIGENCE PEOPLE | 42 |
| VIII. | (A)CCEPTABLE (B)EHAVIOR (C)HANGING ABC TECHNIQUES DESENSITIZATION AND NON-NEED FULFILLMENT STIMULATION | 48 |
| IX. | THE JUDGMENT CALL | 60 |

*Index* .................................................................................................. 71

# WHEN THINKING BEGINS

*Lessons Learned From Helping
Preaverage Intelligence Individuals*

*Chapter I*

# INTRODUCTION

WHEN DOES THINKING BEGIN? My answer is at the point, when for the first time in his life, an individual by his own mental effort corrects a mistake that he appears to be in the process of making. After he has made the error, the correction is more mechanical and procedural. Just prior to commission, it is more dramatic and enlightening. I have reached this conclusion after spending many years of observing and researching the child or adult in all ranges of intelligence, noting particularly the problems of those below average. These people have for many years been called and still are—mentally retarded—a negative terminology.

In March 1972, I published an article entitled *Mental Retardation—Semantically Negative; Preaverage Intelligence—Semantically Positive* in the American Psychological Association Journal *Journal Supplement Abstract Service*. A condensation of this article appeared in the February 1972 issue of the *P C M R Message*, a publication of the President's Commission on Mental Retardation. These publications introduced a new and positive terminology for people in the retardation category. I believe they create new attitudes toward helping them to learn, and as a consequence to become more human, thereby hopefully assisting them to find a place to live in our society like all other people do. I coined the term *preaverage* to remove the negative connotations inherent in the words mentally retarded for the group as a whole and new positive designations for the various subcategories. It is therefore appropriate to launch this book with definitions from my article so as to provide first, a basis for theory, and second, a method for accomplishing the theoretical formulations.

Years of work with intelligence testing, which in my opinion is the greatest single contribution psychology has made to human affairs, has led me to the conclusion that mental retardation developed as a result of a series of possibly unavoidable circumstances. As society became more complex people were observed to behave in strange ways and names were found to describe these conditions. In the area of mental ability, even before an attempt was made to define intelligence, such terms as idiot, imbecile and moron were commonly used.

Today a professional person and others would remain aghast at calling a child of low intelligence an idiot. The term has been effectively removed from the literature after many years and rightly so. Amentia, mental defectiveness and feeblemindedness have also gone their way. Mental retardation has been the overall choice for the past generation with trainable retarded and educable retarded entering the picture. Since however, mental retardation in its most obvious manifestation is a dysfunction in intelligence, no matter what the cause, it would seem time to recognize the unidimensionality of intelligence as a mental trait or perhaps generalized mental function. Thus it would actually appear more prudent to recognize the truth of intelligence differences among individuals and build a scale or terminology that reflects the situation as it really exists.

In the past fifty years, hundreds of many different types of intelligence tests have been given to many millions of individuals. They have always at least divided people into three large groups, above average, average, and below average. In numbered fashion, the popular intelligence quotient or IQ seems to have taken hold beyond the point of eradication. The $Q$ part is especially misleading and should be eliminated. I would prefer intelligence rating, intelligence range, intelligence level or intelligence score. In graphic fashion, the following table shows how in a popular interpretation, people relegate a vertical meaning to intelligence values in daily usage.

This popular and frequently professionally held view places the dimension of intelligence on a vertical or a high-low plane so that those above 90 have all the advantages in our society, while those below have most of the disadvantages including the risk of somehow being captured and placed in institutions. Their only crime is not enough mental ability to cope paradoxically

## TABLE I
### POPULAR INTERACTIVE EFFECT OF INTELLIGENCE VALUES

| Numerical Intelligence Levels | Descriptive Intelligence Levels | |
|---|---|---|
| 110 and up | Above Average | 25% of Population |
| 109 to 90 | Average | 50% of Population |
| 89 or less | Below Average (Mental Retardation Usually at 84 or less) | 25% of Population |

with the standards set by the preponderous other three quarters.

In our country using a figure of 200,000,000 people as the total population, statistical logic would dictate that there are 50,000,000 people below average in intelligence. Since about four or five million retarded have been identified, it means that there are many below average intelligence individuals who manage to do very well. The conclusion to be drawn is that the process of living is more alike for most people than it is different. Therefore, all people have more similarities than differences. But if the view is vertical we have tended to dichotomize or bipolarize the scale of intelligence at point 70, 84 or 90 (take your pick) and push *below average people* into an inferior, even degrading position.

To remedy this, I suggest that we alter our perspective to view all people going forward in a lateral or side by side movement to whatever progressive common goals society creates, with everyone having some chance to share in the accomplishment. My view of the intelligence is unidimensional and more nearly lateral with differences overlapping and at times of minimal importance. Table II as follows illustrates this point of view in simple fashion.

## When Thinking Begins

### TABLE II

#### ALL PEOPLE IN LATERAL POSITION ON THE INTELLIGENCE SCALE

| Preaverage | Average | Above Average |
|---|---|---|
| 10(?) to 89 | 90 to 110 | 111 and up |
| 25% of Population | 50% of Population | 25% of Population |

### NEW TERMINOLOGY AND ITS EFFECT

The lateral view of people side by side on the function of intelligence leads to formulating a new and positive classification for the individuals below average. Currently the designations usually employed with respect to mental retardation are as follows.

### TABLE III

#### WIDELY ACCEPTED INTELLIGENCE RATINGS OF MENTAL RETARDATION

| Score | Numerical Designation | Classification |
|---|---|---|
| 84 - 70 | −1 | Borderline Retardation |
| 69 - 55 | −2 | Mild Retardation |
| 54 - 35 | −3 | Moderate Retardation |
| 34 - 20 | −4 | Severe Retardation |
| 19 or less | −5 | Profound Retardation |

As one can observe this is a vertical designation and has the effect of placing the profound and severely retarded in a limbo of neglect where it is extremely difficult for personnel to feel very rewarded in working with them. In an additional complication the term borderline retardation has the disastrous effect of calling

Introduction 7

people retarded who really are not and can work and accomplish a lot in our society. Many authorities through the years believe that no one with an intelligence score above 70 should ever be called retarded. Borderline Intelligence has frequently been used. It is better but still leaves a nebulous zone in which the border is not clearly related to anything meaningful.

I believe in changing the entire classification system to more positive descriptions and positive numerical ranges arranged in the lateral position.

TABLE IV

BARRETT CLASSIFICATION SYSTEM
FOR PREAVERAGE INTELLIGENCE INDIVIDUALS
(FORMERLY CALLED MENTALLY RETARDED)

| *Approaching Average Intelligence* | *Potential Self-Sufficient Intelligence* | *Emerging Societal Intelligence* | *Self-Care Acquisitional Intelligence* | *Beginning Intelligence* |
|---|---|---|---|---|
| 89-75 (+5) | 74-60 (+4) | 59-45 (+3) | 44-30 (+2) | 29 or less (+1) |

Average intelligence (90 to 110) would be +6 and all the bright people would proceed upward with positive designations which they have always had and enjoyed and which do not present the same types of problems found among preaverage.

In this new classification system, it can be seen that coworkers are more likely to be inspired to devise methods of improving or developing a child with beginning intelligence than one with profound retardation. At present, it is possible to call a human being with an intelligence score of 75, a borderline retardate, a depressing description for probably a capable person. In my system, this same individual could be described as approaching average intelligence, a dynamic forward moving term, away from the polarity of retardation entirely, and more properly thrust into the world of intelligence.

No parent wants to introduce her child as mentally retarded

and many at a great cost to their nervous systems have brought themselves painstakingly to admit this. It would be easier for them and less anxiety producing to have these children recognized as preaverage in intelligence but as possibly whole people otherwise.

*Chapter II*

# THE IMPORTANCE OF INTELLIGENCE

Before one can hope to understand the importance of intelligence for preaverage or retarded people and make a significant or substantial effort to help them, one must thoroughly understand the effect of the distribution of intelligence in our society or in the world. I have noted that mental retardation is basically a problem in low intelligence or what I prefer to call preaverage, therefore I shall take the liberty of using this term throughout the book.

In order to help preaverage individuals a series of variables or conditions must be recognized as interacting dynamic forces. The forces that will be explored in the book comprise the essence of mental ability or what might be called the process of cognitive or conscious mentation. Mentation might be analogous to thinking in its usual form. Many other factors such as memory, motivation, emotionality and so forth also have mentalistic connotations. However the latter are not basically germane to the process of intelligence but coexist in the form of supportive as well as interruptive forces in the total of mentality.

There are many approaches and definitions of intelligence and all are important and quite meaningful. It is a pleasure to credit all my predecessors and contemporaries who have contributed to a knowledge of the field. However for purposes of illustration and explaining my own position on what constitutes intelligence, I must observe a twofold approach to the problem, as I have found that not a single definition thoroughly covers the elusive quality of intelligence. My own approach does not do this without question, either, but at least I think it provides a better base from which to comprehend what a dysfunction of intelligence does to people and why we have institutions and other facilities for individuals full of people whose intelligence seems to be impaired in greater or lesser degree.

I'm going to propose that cognitive mentation or what enables us to know things and use this knowledge effectively is divided into two processes that presumably work closely together yet can experience some degree of distance even though they are housed together as brain functions. The first aspect of cognitive mental ability I shall refer to as *intellect*. Simply stated the intellect is the capacity or ability of mentality to acquire, organize and retain knowledge. Lest one should consider this as an exceptional quality I would point out that subhuman species show intellect. Parakeets can acquire, organize and retain knowledge surprisingly in the form of words. Porpoises and elephants acquire quite a repertoire of intellectual function. In fact so do most animals, maybe all.

The second aspect of mentation is *the intelligence*. This to me is the capacity or ability to solve effectively a new or modified problem or situation the first time a person encounters it. Here is where we human beings may show a difference from other animals in that our intelligence function appears noticeably in our lives while the parakeet may react with unalterable intellect and respond outlandishly to a reasonable cue. Thus the parrot may say "hold the phone" when the pot lid goes up. Fascinating but not an effective exhibition of intelligence.

Intellect and intelligence work together to enable our mental ability to produce appropriate responses so that our bodies and minds can cope with everyday problems. One may indicate that intelligence is the power that pushes or whips the intellect into action. Intelligence generates the strength to enable accumulated knowledge to function properly.

However, under certain conditions, the process breaks down and mistakes, inability to act effectively and confusion may occur. If one can conceive of intelligence as a power factor and intellect as the sum of retained knowledge to which our senses have been exposed, then we can begin to understand what happens mentally to certain people and how to help them. A few observations are in order to help clarify this position.

Perhaps a series of quasi-postulates are in order.

A. Intellect is something put into the brain by exposure to the senses of the body. With sufficient exposure, the knowledge is stored and recalled for use when properly stimulated. Learning that twelve things make a dozen goes into the intellect. Observing for the first time that a clock has a dozen numbers without being told and trying to discover the reason for this represents the emergence of intelligence. If you think your dog is a real bright one, try him on that one.

B. High intelligence predisposes a person to the possibility of accumulating a high intellect.

C. Low intelligence has difficulty acquiring great intellect. (The problem of the retarded or preaverage people).

D. High intelligence may not be motivated or have the opportunity to accumulate high intellect. (An emotional block seen in many college students referred to as HILA or high intelligence, low achiever). However, lack of opportunity seen in the *no book home* to acquire intellect may also occur with high intelligence. Or the *sharp* country boy who can solve anything manual or mechanical but does not have an encyclopedic knowledge.

The purpose in postulating is to focus upon C, namely, that low intelligence does not encourage the accumulation of a store of knowledge or intellect, the basic problem of retardation or preaverage intelligence.

To further understand intelligence and why it is difficult to measure accurately with our present day intelligence tests which really measure intellect, the factor of power alone can be made analogous to a well known electrical equation, called Ohm's Law. It must be remembered that the nervous system is electrochemical in nature, a condition frequently ignored by many psychologists and educators. In fact the real breakthrough in improving intelligence may come through research into the physical nature of this condition.

This illustration is only an analogy and by no means implies that intelligence is electricity. However analogies are useful in clarifying since they can be pictorial and therefore helpful.

In Physics, Ohm's Law states that Amperes $= \dfrac{\text{Voltage}}{\text{Resistance}}$.

Amperes is the something (coulombs) of electricity, and voltage is the power.

Let's simply substitute and we see that the functioning of cognitive mentality may be expressed as follows.

$$\text{Intellect (Amperes?)} = \dfrac{\text{Intelligence (Voltage?)}}{\text{Nervous System Resistance}}.$$

Clearing the equation may produce many interesting variations of acquiring knowledge that may explain cognitive behavior. The analogy is only intended to emphasize to the reader that intelligence is difficult to measure because it is really an unknown power factor and an intelligence voltmeter has not yet been invented. This may explain the many erroneous measurements of intelligence that occur in the preaverage levels. In preaverage individuals, nervous system resistance is easily increased by brain damage, disease, slow reaction time and many other factors. With these people, preferably a test should be culture fair, culture free, universal in item presentation, preferably untimed, standardized from preaverage on through above (not the usual reverse method), nonverbal or symbolic and easily administered with little examiner variable. The search for a measure continues and research will eventually produce the desired instrument so long as all the variables are observed.

So far no tests have been devised to measure this type of nascent power. Consequently we must live with our continued intellectual assessments and their proneness to many errors.

Now putting together these two assumptions, that intelligence is power in the brain and that preaverage individuals have low intellect, inspires an inquiry into a method for increasing this power and at the same time augmenting the knowledge or intellect which may then help to move the child a step further along in its development.

This fundamental theoretical position generated what I have called the ABC method of learning and behavior changing which is intended to improve the position of preaverage people, especially those of beginning intelligence (formerly profoundly retarded), self-care acquisitional intelligence (formerly severely retarded), and emerging societal intelligence (formerly moderately retarded). This is where it is most applicable and most dramatic when it works. It doesn't always do so but my research shows more success than failure. The method is clearly more easily applicable to higher levels such as potentially self-sufficient intelligence (formerly mild retardation) and approaching-average intelligence (formerly borderline retardation). The method is obviously and readily adaptable with normal children.

Throughout the book, I shall use *first level preaverage intelligence* to include beginning intelligence, *self-care acquisitional intelligence* and *emerging societal intelligence*. This corresponds with intelligence ratings of 10 to 55, trainable retarded or lower level retarded. *Second level preaverage intelligence* will refer to those ranges of potentially self-sufficient intelligence and approaching average intelligence or an intelligence rating of 56 to 89, or educable retarded or upper level retarded.

I am sure that after a while you will easily comprehend the system. I had trouble learning it myself and I invented it.

Since the neglected people have been the beginning intelligence, self-care and emerging societal, the emphasis will be placed here. If the method can start this first level preaverage intelligence moving up the ladder of progress, then the second level preaverage intelligence should easily follow.

ABC really means (A)cceptable (B)ehavior (C)hange and was introduced in this day of behavior modification to offset the all encompassing aspects of the latter term. In working with preaverage children many peculiar habits, behavior stereotypes and unusual episodes of conduct must be reasonably changed before a gain can be registered in learning. ABC also implies a graduated step-wise method of learning proceeding simultaneously with behavior changing. The program is esssentially a total stimulation technique created in a residential setting where many helpful forces may converge and permit a good chance for results. Behavior changing employs desensitization techniques, nonneed fulfillment stimulation methods and certain common sense procedures. Both behavior changing and learning techniques work on the principle of immediate reinforcement in the form of mostly positive rewards combined with less emphasis on negative or aversive techniques such as taking the child out of the activity.

The following chapters will describe first the actual method of ABC learning, and, secondly, behavior changing.

*Chapter III*

# THE ABC KEY TO AROUSING OR ALERTING THE DORMANT POWER OF INTELLIGENCE

SINCE THE ASSUMPTION has been made from a theoretical point of view that the ability to know and take the appropriate action is a function of the interaction between intellect and intelligence it follows that these two functions should be developed simultaneously. Most methods of learning and education concentrate on the accumulation of knowledge or intellect. It is difficult at this stage of psychological science to say that intelligence described as a power factor can be created or developed in a certain way. Even though much has been written about the raising and lowering of the IQ, intensive research and study into these experiments show that many hidden variables are at play. In my opinion the intelligence quotient (or IQ) is one thing and intelligence itself is another.

The hypothesis that intelligence tests really measure intellect and then use this measurement to estimate the intelligence predisposes an event or condition which may lead to an almost inevitable error factor. In addition, intellect is clearly an environmental result, whereas intelligence more likely seems predestined by genetic and physiological factors that may permit not a categorically fixed amount of intelligence but possibly a degree of power that may have limitations for flunctuations within a certain range. At any rate the search to increase intelligence continues and the answer may come from a combination of chemical, neurological and psychological research methods. I am therefore not professing to propose a method which will increase intelligence, but a method that may point the way for unleashing the power of intelligence by liberating this force from certain inhibiting factors such as disturbed emotionality, behavior peculiarities, and neurological difficulties that may inhibit its improvement or full potential.

*Acceptable Behavior Change* (ABC) was born because of the need to find ways to deal with the major effect of preaverage intelligence (retardation) which is diminished capacity to generate enough mental power to accumulate intellect. In the first level preaverage ranges this means loss of abstractiveness and ability to shift attention or alertness for quick effective behavior. For preaverage people, the enshrouding problem of life itself is the function of intelligence.

One key toward encouraging intelligence to emerge, from a psychological behavioral learning point of view, is to present stimuli that promote accumulation of intellect at the very simplest level and at the same time direct shift of alertness by being confronted with new or modified situations. In working over a period of years with all types of preaverage individuals from beginning intelligence (profound) to approaching average intelligence (borderline) and from age two up to 30 and 40, I've had the opportunity to conduct experiments with people who like infants in the normal world can be studied from the very beginning of mental development, even though the individuals involved may be six, eight, ten, 12 or 20 years of age. These are persons who have spent a long time in institutions living in situations where mental stimulation was as minimal as possible.

The methods described here have been used many times on people of beginning intelligence (profound), self-care acquisitional intelligence (severe) and emerging societal (moderate) and, of course, higher. But the most dramatic changes are in the beginning group and the self-care.

The system can be demonstrated by a 12-year-old child moved from a living condition where he was not toilet trained, unable to dress or feed himself, cringing with fear at the presence of people, unable to speak a word or gesture meaningfully. He is moved to a renovated residential setting, much less than modern where a total stimulation technique utilizing the services of a Ph.D. psychologist and supporting personnel at varying levels of education and experience are all that is available. The purpose is to determine if it is possible to render this child capable of improving to a point where he can care for himself, demonstrate thought and move on to a higher level of performance. The question is: Can he be turned from an apparent nonentity existence to human? Hopefully after a few months of training, it will be possible to detect some small signs of growth making a prediction possible that at age 18 or 20 he might live outside the institution probably in a sheltered way but even remotely in an almost self-sufficient manner.

He is assigned for eight hours a day to an individual whom we shall call an *in-residence instructor*, who meets almost everyday for an hour or two with the psychologist who works out a total program for the child including every detail of self-care to every facet of mental stimulation. It is in this type of situation that the psychologist discovered that shoe, tin cup and toothbrush are more than articles for walking, drinking and brushing teeth but can be used to start a mental awakening and a system upon which to build the most nascent and rudimentary intellect with the additional fringe benefit of some mental power that might be called intelligence.

B. I. are his initials and this stands for beginning intelligence and the name could refer to a boy or girl since there are many of both in a similar profound category. B. I., even at age 12, unlike normal children, is not eager to learn, not even curious. However positive reinforcement in the form of small marshmallows provide him with motivation as his instructor is taught how to use behavior modification technique slowly but judiciously. B. I. is not feasible for accurate intelligence testing but someone estimated a 20 or so on a type of intelligence scale usually found in most of our institutions.

The psychologist's hypothesis is that stimulation through visual and hearing processes will register in the brain and be retained and an appropriate method will enable these stimuli to emerge as responses in appropriate ways at the right time. It might be added that with sensory stimulation it is not certain that learning may take place. However without stimulation, it is an absolute guarantee not to occur. So by trying there is nothing to lose, only something to gain.

The premise that a starting point for Beginning Intelligence to exhibit itself in a 12-year-old girl or boy who can't talk and whose comprehension and understanding are unknown can be found by integrating the theoretical position of the interaction of intellect and intelligence with a practical application. The theory is that any stimulus exposed to a sensory process such as visual, auditory, or tactile somehow registers an imprint on the brain and is stored away in degree of permanence relatively commensurate with the number and reinforcement of repeated sensations. It is further hypothesized that children like B. I. would naturally be exposed to stimuli that are familiar, real and concrete in nature and not intangible or abstract.

By applying a degree of wisdom, plus some trial and error, it developed that the three most common objects exposed visually to our children of beginning intelligence, and this may be true in most American homes, was a shoe, a cup and a toothbrush. These are the real objects that are used daily. There are many realistic toy facsimiles of hundreds of life's objects that will be used later on in the ABC process of learning. The shoe is actually a tennis shoe about 5 inches long, 2 inches wide and an inch or two high. Its color is reasonably unimportant but red or white is preferred. The cup is real and used for drinking purposes on the daily basis. It is made out of tin or aluminum so as to be unbreakable. In working with people with beginning intelligence most objects must be made of indestructible quality. The cup measures about 3½ inches in height and the same diameter. These articles need not be precise in measurement because at this stage exact size is not a crucial variable. The toothbrush is simply an ordinary toothbrush of good size but not overly large (approximately 5½ inches is a good length).

Before beginning the instructing process, several factors have to be cleared. The child should be able to hear reasonably well otherwise if there is any degree of deafness a different approach will have to be used. The child should have enough arm and hand mobility to be able to point to the objects, be able to feel the objects, be able to pick them up, be able to hold them and be able to hand them to the instructor. Any one or all of these actions may be necessary for crediting correct identification.

Pictures of objects are not suitable at this stage because they represent symbols or abstractions and are therefore stimulating the weakest mental aspects of preaverage people, namely the inability to abstract or think symbolically. This stage of development will come later if it is reached at all with beginning intelligence. If it does the child will have made a great mental gain and be on its way to humanization. Let's return to our beginning stimulation the first time it was ever done with B. I. the ABC way.

It is assumed in an ABC method that a stepwise or graduated form of learning occurs on a scale of increasing difficulty that is reasonably equal from item to item. This actually is impossible because we are not dealing with objects that can be measured in inches or pounds but which portray differences that must be estimated logically at first, then verified empirically, if possible. In other words, a series of presentations begins at A and hopefully proceeds upward in its mental challenging value to B, to C, to D and etc. In addition, such intangibles as familiarity of object, reality level and abstractive potential must be considered. Tangible qualities such as weight, width, depth and size must also be evaluated.

In psychology the familiar concept of *just noticeable difference* or JND plays an important role in establishing the difficulty level of items. So too, in the ABC method, the very crucial aspect of the learning process is to achieve a series of items where the B Series is just noticeably different or one JND removed from A. This is an impossible thing to do especially since our above average intelligence people are attempting to arrange the stimuli for preaverage individuals. Nonetheless it is possible to approximate the distances and establish by research their relative value. The ones presented here have been evaluated by working many times with many individuals at the beginning to approaching average levels of intelligence. Our point of concentration is upon first level preaverage individuals (10 to 55).

Measurements below 10 are ridiculous; in fact 10 is bad enough. If substantial progress can occur in this range, the method with sufficiently increasing stimulation will produce results for second level preaverage individuals (56 to 89). It is much easier to work with high or second level preaverage than with first level.

The attention span of a beginning intelligence child like B. I.

is extremely restricted. Afterall B. I. is hyperactive, sensitive, nervous, easily distracted, possibly on the autistic side. At first B. I. cannot attend for more than ten or fifteen minutes. As a matter of fact, experimentation soon reveals that direct one to one learning or brain work sessions in a private secluded room cannot exceed ten percent of an hour or six minutes of real optimally alert mental stimulation. But this much net time for intensive brain stimulation twice a day has been found to produce desired results. The remainder of the eight-hour daytime is occupied with a variety of stimulating activities, relaxation periods, passive learning and other activities, some designed to render purposive results, others intended only to continue routines and provide a surrounding milieu fertile enough to be conducive to humanistic growth. Naturally the atmosphere is relaxed, leisurely, and homelike with music, television and stories in the background or forefront as B. I.'s needs may suggest.

The Barrett ABC technique is a combination of elements of several theories, some play therapy and facets of behavior modification. Positive immediate reinforcement in the form of candy when necessary and verbal praise later is the motivational foundation.

When it is known that a child like B. I. may not have experienced any direct learning in his life, a basic or fundamental series of items is presented in a certain way. Experience has taught that fifteen items in combinations of three are sufficient to maintain learning sessions for possibly days or weeks.

In essence, it works like this. The basic or beginning series for first time beginning intelligence is as follows. The principle involved is that first, a thing must be presented visually to the brain and then placed in a situation where it can be recognized by an exertion of brain power which discriminates the object in a variety of settings which are new or modified and which proceed from familiar widely different combinations to less familiar and more tightly related, so as to exercise effort and not just memory. In the basic or beginning series of fifteen, daily familiarity and commonality of the objects is more a variable than anything else. The just noticeable difference if one exists from A to B to C to D to E is questionable but workable.

## ABC Key to Alerting Dormant Power

In the Barrett ABC method combination, A is always the easiest and most different and B represents a mental advance of a small degree. Theoretically this would make the 26th step Z, the most difficult and the top of the ladder. Therefore in writing, A should be at the bottom of a series and proceed upward. But people, not just preaverage, have a hard time thinking this way, so with the reader's understanding and indulgence, we show A at the top of the page and E at the bottom. Because of the six to ten minute alertness limitation it is not necessary to program beyond E but to start a whole new grouping of series of items. This enables the instructor to know where to begin, how low for beginning intelligence, how high for potential self sufficient intelligence.

The standard method of presentation of objects is always horizontal.

### STANDARD HORIZONTAL ARRANGEMENT

Shoe    Cup    Toothbrush

### PRIMARY FIRST STEP CHOICE DISCRIMINATION GROUP FOR FIRST LEVEL PREAVERAGE INTELLIGENCE INDIVIDUALS

#### Familiar Objects

A. Shoe    Cup    Toothbrush
   (a-1)  (a-2)   (a-3)

  B. Comb   Glass   Spoon
     (b-1)   (b-2)   (b-3)

    C. Soap   Sock   Bowl
       (c-1)   (c-2)   (c-3)

      D. Toothpaste tube  Safety pin  Baby
          (d-1)          (d-2)    powder can
                                        (d-3)

        E. Clock   Telephone   Chair
           (e-1)    (e-2)     (e-3)

22                     *When Thinking Begins*

This primary series was purposely designed to find objects common to home, institutional settings or hospitals and possible other types of environments. It also must be remembered that B. I. at twelve years of age cannot talk and we have no way of knowing the first time what he may comprehend. A cup or toothbrush in A may be a daily affair but what use does B. I. have for a *clock* or *telephone* at the E level. This series of fifteen items took B. I. better than a month of daily sessions to learn in the choice situations.

The instructor is taught to assume that B. I. is not capable of distinguishing anything correctly. So when combination A is presented, the instructor introduces each item one at a time in order from B. I.'s left to his right because this is the way he may read someday. The instructor preferably sits beside B. I. on his right, close to him because this allows the instructor to comfort him with her left arm if necessary (human touch appropriately and skillfully performed is very reassuring) and present the items one at a time with her more skillful right hand.

The objects should be carefully arranged and prepared ahead of time and kept in a container preferably on the instructor's right side at waist level and out of sight. In the pocket of her uniform on the right she must always be prepared with her material rewards, candy corn, mints, cereals, all colorful, easily swallowed and easy to use. Correct responses only are rewarded and on the incorrect choices the instructor remains neutral. The middle object; an unbreakable cup, is placed fourteen to sixteen inches away from B. I.'s nose, the shoe two to three inches to the left of the cup and the toothbrush, two to three inches to its right. This arrangement gives B. I. the optimum visual perceptual overall or Gestalt point of view. He must be given all of the advantages possible because it is never really known how well his eyes focus, what brain damage does to his perception or whether his hands can perform what his eyes direct him to do.

The cardinal rule in work with all preaverage intelligence individuals (or formerly all retarded persons) is that an unknown variable may spoil a situation. Put into adage form, this means that for want of a shoe a horse was lost and so on. In other words

B. I. may know, but a little circumstance such as objects too close, too far, may blur the correctness of the response.

The instructor introduces the shoe by its name and keeps repeating it in several different ways. This is called entering the intellect by sensory stimulation and hopefuly starting to build it. The instructor says "Here's a shoe" or "See the shoe," or "Touch the shoe" or "Hold the shoe" or "Point to the shoe," by grasping B. I.s hand and creating the familiar index finger point with his hand inside the instructor's. "You know, B.I., you wear shoes on your feet," "You don't hurt your feet walking on the ground with them," etc., creating a rather constant chatter to provide auditory stimulation which may someday return in the form of verbal knowledge from B. I. himself. This rather constant chatter is very important towards acculturating children. It is one of the most readily neglected activities of a parent or an instructor. Being a grown woman or man, the instructor feels silly doing it. But ridiculous or not, it should go on all day long in a variety of ways with many different things provided in our total stimulation environment. Total stimulation as a spontaneous and structured technique will be discussed in a latter chapter.

It is now assumed that B. I. sees the shoe and has heard the word. The same thing is repeated with the cup with chatter appropriate to it, and then with the toothbrush and words suitable to it. Now he is ready for the first combination of three objects in which to exercise choice discrimination. Three are chosen because experimentation has indicated that two objects only allows too much of a guessing game with an even chance of correctness and restricted use of changing position of objects (permutation) or other combinations. Four and five are too many and cumbersome for both child and instructor, at least in working with first level preaverage intelligence individuals. Three has proven to be optimum allowing six permutations and new combinations and less guessing.

B. I. looks at the three objects as they are placed in front of him and the instructor says "Touch the shoe" or "Give me the cup" or "Hold the toothbrush," whatever seems proper to encourage B. I. to respond. If he correctly touches the cup or hands it over, he receives immediately a reward of candy. If he hands an object to an instructor, it is replaced so that a choice is always made from three things at a time. This is important to the system. When B. I. has gotten all three things correctly, permutation in two or three positions are tried and correctness obtained before moving to row *B*. In fact each time B. I. correctly identifies an item, the object is replaced in a different position.

Row *B* objects, comb, glass (plastic), spoon may be taught as in *A*. However, it has been discovered that what is termed a *lead into familiarity* is more effective and may reduce any frustration incurred by moving on too fast. Such frustration is to be avoided if possible. Thus a new combination is possible with the already known shoe and cup by combining spoon with them. Again this combination may be used with comb and glass. As the items proceed to advance, many combinations become possible thus producing new and modified situations where according to our definition, intelligence may emerge and thinking can literally be seen to operate.

B. I. proceeds painstakingly to items in *C*, *D*, and *E* until after almost a month he knows all fifteen objects in almost any combination or permutation, our only way of proving he knows because he doesn't talk. For the first time in his life, he has exhibited what may be the ingredients of intelligence, namely discrimination, differentiation, contrast and compare or what I like to call the DDCC principle, my idea of the essence of learning. Discrimination to distinguish finer and finer nuances, differentiation to find identifying differences, contrast to determine important opposites, and compare to find similarities that are helpful. DDCC makes the brain work and enables it to transfer power to other situations when they are changed or new.

Recombining items permits an examination of the ability to discriminate more minute differences, an exercise that promotes strength for the power of intelligence. At this simple level in this basic series, the instructor may combine the aluminum cup from *A*, the aluminum cereal bowl from *C* and the aluminum *glass* from *B* and produce in essence a very tight combination of much sameness, at least to a little boy or girl whose intelligence someone tried to estimate at 20 something.

If B. I. identifies them correctly, the instructor moves to different levels. If not, she may take a step backward so that B. I. experiences success and reward. In other words, frustrating levels are not permitted to reduce motivation for long as they tend to be regressive. So just as the *A combination*, to the *B triad*, to the *C trio* moves forward and upward, so the *C* combination to *B* to *A* moves backward and reviews. The general approach made by this first level of preaverage intelligence children is never steadily upward but a series of zig-zagging efforts or possibly a back and forth effort like the ribs of an accordion. However, as B. I. succeeds eventually, he seems to go farther forward and much less backward. B. I.'s progress may be charted at $A$, $B$—back to $B$ but not $A$—then $B$, $C$, $D$—back to $D$, $C$ but not $B$ then forward to $C$, $D$, $E$ and ready for the next advanced group of stimulus objects. Lower case letters and numbers serve to indicate the level of the item for ready programming and recording purposes.

### Related Phenomena

Sometimes a child like B. I., or it may happen at all levels of intelligence, will encounter a plateau effect or stop at a certain combination and not be able to advance.

Let's assume it happens for B. I. at $E$, Clock, Telephone, Chair. Arrangement from left to right, right to left, center, right, left, etc. are tried and he still doesn't get them all. We know that preaverage or brain damaged frequently show intellectual rigidity or an inability to shift perception to a new set or way. So the instructor tries a different arrangement. Thus she may arrange the items straight in front of B. I.'s nose, called a Vertical Approach. Or in graphic form as follows.

VERTICAL APPROACH
Chair
Telephone
Clock

The first item is about 12 inches in front of B. I.'s face, the next about 15 inches and the chair about 18 inches. This still doesn't produce the desired result. So a Left Diagonal Arrangement is tried, then a Right Diagonal. Graphically like this.

### LEFT DIAGONAL ARRANGEMENT

Chair

        Telephone

                Clock

### RIGHT DIAGONAL ARRANGEMENT

                Chair

        Telephone

Clock

Distances about the same as before and same reference point. If there is still no result a Left-Sided Configuration is tried like this.

### LEFT-SIDED CONFIGURATION

        Chair

Telephone

        Clock

or a Right-Sided Configuration such as this.

        Chair

                Telephone

        Clock

It has happened a number of times that these shifts will break the blocks and surprisingly correctness occurs. This is particularly interesting in that visual changes or shift of perception may play a role here. Regardless of explanation, it enables an advance and certainly is worth the effort.

### Continuation Of The Various Groupings
### That Have Been Tried For First Level Intelligence Individuals

Each grouping presented represents an upward advance. Many groups are possible after one understands the underlying principle; that is combination of three objects, pictures, abstractions, etc. from a widely different relationship to very closely related combinations. Many of the objects are purchased in stores, ordered from educational supply firms, or made by our own ingenuity. All objects should be as realistic in appearance as possible. A cow standing on her back legs, with pink bells on her front feet, a blue bonnet on her head, pink bows on her horns and a silly unnatural grin is not the way to introduce this animal to a child of beginning intelligence (profoundly retarded) for the first time in his life. It is confusing and misleading. Later on he can react to this as a lead toward abstractions.

## SECOND STEP CHOICE DISCRIMINATION GROUP
## FOR FIRST LEVEL PREAVERAGE INTELLIGENCE INDIVIDUALS

### Vegetable Group

A. Potato     Cucumber     Carrot
    (a-1)        (a-2)        (a-3)

B. Bell pepper     Onion     Sweet potato
    (b-1)        (b-2)        (b-3)

C. Green squash     Turnip     Tomato
    (c-1)        (c-2)        (c-3)

D. Dried Field Peas     Dried soup beans     Dried corn kernels
    (d-1)        (d-2)        (d-3)

E. Trimmed, radish     Trimmed, red beet     Pimento pepper
    (e-1)        (e-2)        (e-3)

Same procedure for introduction of items is used here and again the hypothesis of advancing from a widely different relationship in the A combination to a closely related variable in E is maintained. If a child responds to an object with a different name other than the one given here, such as vernacular, colloquialism or *nickname*, its correctness must be judged and rewarded or not as the response may indicate.

## THIRD STEP CHOICE DISCRIMINATION GROUP
## FOR FIRST LEVEL PREAVERAGE INTELLIGENCE INDIVIDUALS

### Fruit Group

A. Apple     Banana     Lemon
    (a-1)        (a-2)       (a-3)

    B. Orange     Pear     Peach
       (b-1)        (b-2)     (b-3)

       C. Raspberries     Strawberries     Blackberries
          (c-1)             (c-2)            (c-3)

          D. Cherries     Grapes     Olives
             (d-1)         (d-2)     (d-3)

             E. Small     Small     Apricot
                beige      tannish     (e-3)
                plum      persimmon
                (e-1)       (e-2)

## FOURTH STEP ADVANCE CHOICE DISCRIMINATION GROUP
## FOR FIRST LEVEL PREAVERAGE INTELLIGENCE INDIVIDUALS

### Common Household Objects—Realistic Toy Form

A. Table     Toilet     Chair
    (a-1)       (a-2)       (a-3)

    B. Bed     Television     Table lamp
       (b-1)        (b-2)        (b-3)

       C. Spoon     Fork     Knife
          (c-1)        (c-2)     (c-3)

          D. Frying pan     Pitcher     Egg beater
             (d-1)           (d-2)       (d-3)

             E. Ladle     Pancake     Serving
                (e-1)       turner      spoon
                           (e-2)        (e-3)

## ABC Key to Alerting Dormant Power

### FIFTH STEP ADVANCE CHOICE DISCRIMINATION GROUP FOR FIRST LEVEL PREAVERAGE INTELLIGENCE INDIVIDUALS

#### Common Animals

A. Horse    Squirrel    Dog
   (a-1)      (a-2)     (a-3)

B. Cow    Pig    Cat
   (b-1)   (b-2)   (b-3)

C. Bull    Calf    Colt
   (c-1)   (c-2)   (c-3)

D. Sheep    Goat    Deer
   (d-1)    (d-2)   (d-3)

E. Rabbit    Skunk    Racoon
   (e-1)     (e-2)    (e-3)

### SIXTH STEP ADVANCE CHOICE DISCRIMINATION GROUP FOR FIRST LEVEL PREAVERAGE INTELLIGENCE INDIVIDUALS

#### Less Familiar Household Objects

A. Tea kettle    Soup pot    Sauce pan
    (a-1)       (a-2)      (a-3)

B. Sofa    Cupboard    Day Bed
   (b-1)     (b-2)      (b-3)

C. Table    Buffet    Cabinet
   (c-1)    (c-2)    (c-3)

D. Wash basin    Dressing table    Bathtub
    (d-1)        (d-2)        (d-3)

E. Stove    Sink cabinet    Refrigerator
   (e-1)     (e-2)      (e-3)

## SEVENTH STEP ADVANCE CHOICE DISCRIMINATION GROUP
## FOR FIRST LEVEL PREAVERAGE INTELLIGENCE INDIVIDUALS

### Wild Animal Group

A. Lion    Monkey    Elephant
  (a-1)    (a-2)    (a-3)

B. Tiger    Zebra    Hippopotamus
  (b-1)    (b-2)    (b-3)

C. Bear    Giraffe    Kangaroo
  (c-1)    (c-2)    (c-3)

D. Moose    Antelope    Elk
  (d-1)    (d-2)    (d-3)

E. Panther    Bobcat    Puma
  (e-1)    (e-2)    (e-3)

## EIGHTH STEP ADVANCE CHOICE DISCRIMINATION GROUP
## FOR FIRST LEVEL PREAVERAGE INTELLIGENCE INDIVIDUALS

### Vehicle Group

A. Train    Truck    Boat
  (engine)    (a-2)    (a-3)
  (a-1)

B. Bus    Train    Van
  (b-1)    (flat car)    (truck)
             (b-2)    (b-3)

C. Sedan auto    Stationwagon    Truck
  (c-1)    (c-2)    (loading)
                             (c-3)

D. Firetruck    Wrecker    Jeepster
  (d-1)    (d-2)    (d-3)

E. Cement    Tractor    Dumptruck
  mixer    trailer    (e-3)
  truck    truck
  (e-1)    (e-2)

*ABC Key to Alerting Dormant Power* 31

NINTH STEP ADVANCE CHOICE DISCRIMINATION GROUP
FOR FIRST LEVEL PREAVERAGE INTELLIGENCE INDIVIDUALS

## Less Familiar Common Objects

A. Pin    Button    Rubber band
    (a-1)     (a-2)     (a-3)

B. Pocket knife    Nail clipper    Nail file
    (b1-)     (b-2)     (b-3)

C. Paint brush    Hair brush    Nail brush
    (c-1)     (c-2)     (c-3)

D. Magazine    Paper    Book
    (d-1)     (news)     (d-3)
                (d-2)

E. Crayon    Pencil    Chalk
    (e-1)     (e-2)     (e-3)

*Chapter IV*

# THE ABC ONE VARIABLE APPROACH

WHAT TO DO when a child completes all of the actual object series (which B. I. has not done as yet) or to work with second level intelligence individuals is explained by slowly moving into abstractions or symbols in the form of pictures or symbols. Everything presented so far may be obtained in picture, meaning realistic photograph form and presented and worked with in the same way. We have prepared literally hundreds of pictures in series form but they are too voluminous for presentation here. However color and common shapes are so essential to living that they must be given special treatment and emphasis. B. I. and many others are ready for some phase of color or form, varying from simple to more complex.

In order to assure the best chance of getting good responses and making sure the child knows, all cues except one should be eliminated to teach color and form. All series should begin with the most familiar and basic and proceed to less familiar and more complex.

If for the first time in his life, B. I. is shown a bright red ball (size of a tennis ball) alongside of a green block or cube (about the same size) he will begin to point correctly to the red one or green one. This does not mean he knows his colors because there are other cues or variables in operation. So to make sure he learns, we make cards which present only a certain color in a certain form, or a real block in one color, and identically the same size block in another color.

Again with first level preaverage intelligence individuals, the four so-called primary strong colors are presented preferably in our usual manner of three at a time. These colors are real red, blue, yellow and green. We make a white background cardboard about four inches on each side with a solid red square in

# The ABC One Variable Approach

the center of it about two inches on each side. We make many cards like this with the same size green square, blue square or yellow square. We also add many cards of the same square shape and size with circles in the center about two inches in diameter also colored the same red, yellow, green and blue. We create these cards with triangles in all of these colors with the perpendicular from apex to base two inches high and the base two inches wide. This is reasonable size approximation.

Finally cards with rectangles in the four colors, two inches high and one and a half times as wide to obtain a JND (just noticeable difference) from the square. This is consistent with forcing the power of intelligence to emerge and solve a problem. Actually concerning the rectangle we shall not leave B. I. unable to see the difference at one and a half times, but will move up gradually toward double width to obtain success if necessary.

To illustrate our one variable procedure for teaching color, we shall demonstrate the method graphically.

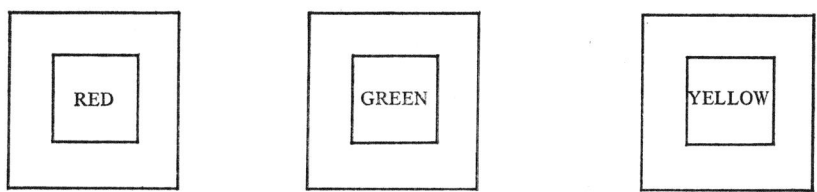

Once again choice discrimination procedure with material reward like candy will be used unless verbal reinforcement is sufficient.

As usual the colors are introduced by name with constant repetition and then placed into the series. The instructor says, "Show me red," "Point to red," "Pick up red" or whatever is necessary to obtain response. It will be noted that the only cue or variable is color since all the forms are squares. Again after a correct response is made, the object is replaced in a different position so as to insure the accuracy of his knowledge.

After these colors are known the blue square card is substituted for one in the series and it is positively reinforced into the intellect.

After these colors are known (and B. I. hasn't gotten this far) then black and white are introduced. Appropriate cards are made for black and white.

Second level intelligence may go beyond the primaries, so hues of brown, purple and orange are used in card form next. If these are known and accomplished then tints like pink, tan, orchid, aqua, gold and gray are worked with in the same manner.

For all preaverage intelligence levels, series of colors are repeated using circles, triangles and rectangles. In addition if the symbolism of the card is too abstract, the same principle is applied to three dimensional objects using specially prepared block, balls, etc.

To teach shape or form, the one variable approach is again used with the same cards. The graphic presentation is like this.

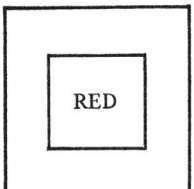 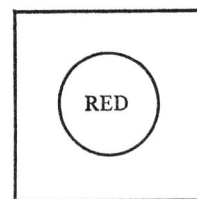 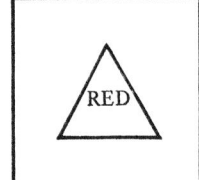

It will be noticed that the only cue is shape since all colors are red on white background. Now the instructor follows the same choice discrimination method. She introduces the idea of square (it may be called something different), circle and then triangle. The rectangle is last to be introduced because of its conflicting relationship with the square. First level preaverage intelligence individuals may grasp the difference in square, circle, triangle but not proceed too much further.

It is possible to go up to more complex level with second level preaverage intelligence individuals. Indeed for the some of these there may not be a real limit on the complexity. We suggest the following order of approach. Using real tridimensionals.

Cube—Oval—Pyramid<br>
Sphere—Cylinder—Cone

On painting cards with two-dimensions, the shape progression is as follows.

Trapezoid—Rhomboid—Pentagon<br>
Hexagon—Heptagon—Octagon

Beyond eight sides a figure may become too circular even for a child in the approaching average intelligence level and frustration may set in. This must be worked with carefully and ingeniously.

### Indefinite Uses of Choice Discrimination

Choice discrimination as a method to store intellect and challenge intelligence has no fixed groupings, series or special presentations that must be strictly observed. Every child or person must be individually programmed for best results and constant readjustment is necessary. Many combinations can be devised and for second level preaverage intelligence individuals when the world of abstractions is reached, the possibilities for presentations are limitless. The prime requisite is that the instructors have resourcefulness, a warm heart and infinite patience. It is not possible to help all preaverage but the method shows promise of obtaining more successes than failures when properly applied.

Obviously for greater difficulty and challenge as needed, the method may include the use of the function of objects and pictures and continue to the more abstract use of the familiar analogy or similarity of the three objects.

*Chapter V*

# THE IMPORTANCE OF THE BARRETT ABC METHOD OF DIRECTIONS IN SETTING THE STAGE FOR LEARNING

IT IS AXIOMATIC IN LEARNING that one must direct attention or alertness, at least in varying degrees, to something before it can effectively be recorded in the intellect and remain there for accurate recall. Can attention be taught? This is almost an absurd question to ask. Generally it is taken for granted more or less with normal people. However, when dealing with mentally retarded whom I now call preaverage intelligence individuals, especially at the beginning levels, the question is not so redundant but assumes great importance. Ask any special education teacher or mother of a retarded child.

Focusing attention, no matter how long or short, is a necessary stage for learning. In the ABC method we have found that directions (some people call them commands) can be used if they are carefully planned and positively reinforced. Our experimental work with preaverage at all levels has focused upon verbal instructions of certain kinds and in certain degrees of complexity. It is obvious that for this to succeed, the child must be able to hear. Practice in directions really should precede choice discrimination or any other activity. However, like anything else with children of beginning intelligence, there is never a right time to do certain things but only an opportune time when the alertness of the instructor indicates it is time to try directions.

Directions involve abstractions and memory both in the words that are used and in what needs to be accomplished. B. I. is still in the single direction or simple command stage. He is trying very hard to move into the *two-idea* direction stage but is having difficulty. For example, a single idea direction such as "Eat your peas" is easy enough for B. I. after all, he does have a good appetite. When the direction is formalized, however, by starting him from a certain point in a room and sending him about ten feet away to bring an object back, he can finally accomplish this but not too easily. The direction is as follows "Go over to that chair, and bring back the block." He is rewarded for accomplishing this.

The instructor moves on to a *two idea* direction such as "Pick up your toy and put it on the table." B. I. begins to hesitate but after a long time of practice, he can achieve the desired goal.

After many months, the instructor attempts a *three idea* direction and encounters difficulty. A toothbrush is placed on a chair in one corner of the room, and about ten feet straight across on another chair a block is positioned. B. I. is stationed about twelve feet in front and in the middle of the two objects. The directions are to go the chair on his left, get the toothbrush, then over to the one on his right for the block and bring them both back to his instructor. B. I. cannot quite accomplish this so some adjustments are made.

Sometimes experience has shown that if the visual perceptual field is reduced in size, the child can more readily see the objects. So the two chairs are moved with their objects about five feet apart, about eight feet in front of B. I. Some children succeed in this way and then the distance is increased again before moving to possible *four idea* directions which are quite difficult for *first level intelligence* except at the *emerging societal range* (formerly moderately retarded).

A *four idea* direction is one like the following. "Take the waste basket outside and empty it in the trash can." The four ideas, easy for normals, include (1) take the waste basket (2) outside (door open) (3) empty it (4) in trash can.

Training in directions is an important part of learning for pre-average children if they are to achieve in school, work or in general survive with a degree of routine and regularity in their lives. Following directions in a sense disciplines the intelligence power so that intellect may be accumulated under controlled circumstances.

*Chapter VI*

# THE VALUE OF THE JIGSAW PUZZLE IN ITS VARIOUS ROLES IN THE MENTAL DEVELOPMENT OF PREAVERAGE INTELLIGENCE INDIVIDUALS

THE JIGSAW PUZZLE has been on the American scene for a long time as a source of entertainment or pastime for young and old. To a group of adults a one thousand piece puzzle is not alarming or unconquerable but a challenge for an evening or two or longer. Besides they've got the picture to look at.

Beginning intelligence children can also do jigsaw puzzles but they must preferably be a certain type and made in a particular way. The best are those that are constructed in a real sturdy way of thick wooden or plastic inlaid pieces contained in a heavy supporting background. They should be brightly colored with themes or ideas that appeal to children and follow the general rule in working with preaverage intelligence children, that is, to be as close to reality as possible.

An elephant standing on a red barrel on one hind leg, twirling a blue baton in his trunk, with golden bells on his ears and a little monkey laughing on his back, does not present a true picture to the beginning intelligence children of a real elephant when seen especially for the first time. This is true in jigsaw puzzles as well as objects for choice discrimination. Very realistic ones are hard to find but may be made and are well worth the effort. However, some degree of unreality may be permitted in jigsaw puzzles if it is not too greatly distorted and too early in the series.

With first level preaverage intelligence children, the ABC method assumes that the simplest puzzle must be used first and proceed piece by piece up the ladder of difficulty. In essence, then, the simplest is a one-piece single in which only a dog or cat is placed in the middle of the board and that is all. The first time a child accomplishes this, a reward is in order, preferably as always verbal praise, hand clapping, but candy if necessary. Next a two-piece single or separate is presented.

To interject at this point, the puzzles in which a complete figure, animal, house or tree appears as one piece fitting into its own slot is referred to as *single or separate*. These generally range from one-piece separates to seven-piece separates. The other type where two pieces or more are cut to fit snugly adjacent to each other and complete an item, such as peach, engine or hat when properly placed are called adjacents. The adjacent series generally range from a two-piece to thirty one-piece. This is enough for first level intelligence but, of course, for second level intelligence, fifty, hundred-piece and up are available. There are higher level preaverage who can do four hundred or five hundred-piece puzzles more quickly than we *normal* people.

The puzzles are carefully sorted and named. The criteria for determining difficulty is basically, that the more pieces in the puzzle, the more intricate it is. However, while this is a major variable and easily used conversationally for ready identification, it can be misleading. For example, a four-piece adjacent *apple* all in one solid color with no lines or shading can be more difficult than a six-piece adjacent picture of a boy in four different colors. If pieces have guide lines to each other, the puzzle is easier. If the picture is more realistic, it can be less difficult. The way in which pieces are cut can vary the difficulty level and so can the total configuration.

In use the child is helped, if necessary, since he does not look at a completed picture while doing the puzzle. When he can put it all together by himself, he moves on usually to a second one with the same number of pieces, and then after accomplishing this one, he goes up to the next series of puzzles, one piece more complex. So this requires our just noticeable difference (JND) or applying ABC gradation to jigsaw puzzles.

B. I. is a classical example of steady painstaking progress. It has taken him about forty weeks working fifteen to thirty minutes a day to accomplish the seven singles, plus eighteen adjacents, advancing one piece at a time. He is now working carefully on his nineteen-piece adjacent. His rate of advance on puzzles is slower than typical for first level preaverage intelligence children but when one reflects that about a year ago, he didn't do any, wasn't even toilet trained and was custodially sheltered, his progress is sure and steady. With his hair nicely groomed, a less frightened look and neatly dressed, he begins to exhibit the poise of a young boy even in the midst of a fragile nervous system.

Why are puzzles so important to our ABC Program? I personally do not believe they add too much to the power of intelligence because their reasoning is none too logical and trial and error is an easy out. Nonetheless we could not do without them because of the following reasons.

1. Jigsaw puzzles comprise the glue or mental cement that holds other parts of the program together. They do this for both instructor and child. Instructors also have to have a respite from very confining and exacting work especially with children of first level preaverage intelligence. The puzzle is self-contained requiring little preparation.

2. The jigsaw puzzle is something that has a visible beginning and an ending which fits into the completeness and wholeness desire of both instructor and child. Unlike other activities, it can be finished, viewed and admired. It is in essence an accomplishment which can be done in a limited amount of time and most people like to get things done.

3. It is a good inanimate instructor of a part-whole approach and can teach how small pieces can grow into something big and recognizable. This is self-motivating in that it compels or drives the individual performing the puzzle to persist in finishing it. Since first level preaverage intelligence individuals do not find drive and motivation from within, it must be supplied from forces outside the person, and this type of puzzle does that.

4. It provides a self-corrective form of reasoning even though in a trial and error fashion. In other words, a child can readily see that a piece doesn't fit and change to another just by hunting for it. In this sense intelligence is not overtaxed or overdriven.

5. It is a form of reasoning favoring a concrete approach over

the abstractive. The answer is there somewhere in those pieces and can be found by a combination of hands and mind, something very important to preaverage intelligence people who have difficulty abstracting an answer that is purely mental.

In summation the jigsaw puzzle is of inestimable value for gaining the attention of preaverage people from the very early beginning intelligence category on up to the approaching average intelligence range.

*Chapter VII*

## A TOTAL STIMULATION ENVIRONMENT FOR PREAVERAGE INTELLIGENCE PEOPLE

THE FOREGOING PROGRAM presented the heart of a method intended primarily to unleash the intelligence power and build the intellect through the adaptation of simple means that have been found to be effective with the very beginning end of the intelligence scale. The same methods with increasing intricacy and complexity can be employed all the way up the scale of intelligence, even to average and above average people.

However, there is more to an eight-hour-day than self-care instruction, choice discrimination, directions and puzzles. In fact this may fill up only a few hours. A little more time is spent with behavior change programming to be described later. The remaining time must be filled in with other designed activities such as music, drawing, painting, play outdoor and indoor, television, radio and reading. All of these activities must be blended into a simple yet complex cultural milieu that can best be described by the term *total stimulation*.

This means that a learning and behavior changing environment is created in a home-like milieu which permits personnel to function leisurely with a minimum of pressure and be constantly with the children for the eight prime hours of the day. In this type of setting where certain activities already described can be called structured, certain nonprescribed and nonstructured activities may be used to occupy time, to further instruction or to change behavior in a more casual and acceptable way.

The tasks to be employed vary all the way from simple coloring of a ball, to a giraffe, to the outline of a famous person or even to an outline of the Taj Mahal. This in a simple way describes a totally stimulating visual occurrence which along with appropriate *chatter* and conversation may serve to enable two senses; vision and hearing, to help build an intellect which is challenging and uplifting. This theory assumes that total stimulation may eventually render a gain toward the abstract which is vitally important for mental survival in our society. When the conversation of the drawing centers around the importance of the famous man or the unique beauty of the Taj Mahal, then ideas and words have a chance of registering on the brain and may emerge perhaps in a different form as the child grows and improves. As stated previously, bi-sensory stimulation may not achieve anything in the long run for first level preaverage intelligence individuals but without being exposed to it there is absolute certainty that the brain will gain nothing. In a learning situation like this, even a small advance means everything—a total loss leaves only the previous status quo.

The same method is followed with music varying from stimulation with Mother Goose Rhymes and songs of animals up to lullabys, then to Strauss' Waltzes, maybe "Peter and the Wolf" or "The Nutcracker Suite" and, indeed, Beethoven's Fifth Symphony. Much of this music is played in the background as other things go on. Sometimes it is rendered for a definite purpose. One child of beginning intelligence is restless when "Old MacDonald Had A Farm" is played but becomes very quiet, tractable, and amenable listening to "Peter and the Wolf."

The same concept applied to music is followed in reading stories. The *Three Little Bears* with many others at this level may occasionally be followed by parts of the daily newspaper, a little of *Tom Sawyer* or *Lincoln's Gettysburg Address*. These readings can also be direct at certain times or in the background on tapes or recordings. In total stimulation technique the learning can be active or passive. Even learning while asleep can be considered under properly monitored conditions and proper equipment.

Total stimulation extends to establishing certain visual techniques that can be talked about by the instructors several times a day, every day, in many different ways. The windows and walls should be covered with very real replicas in picture form of such objects as The American Flag, The Statue of Liberty, and

The U.S. Capitol Building. The windows and walls might also include The Praying Hands, an elephant, a camel, a fish, an eagle, a schoolhouse, famous people like George Washington, Abraham Lincoln, Booker T. Washington, George Washington Carver, flowers, a baseball, etc. Alongside or underneath every picture should be space enough to place pictures that have been drawn by the children no matter how poor the attempt.

Spaces in a total stimulation program should be shared on a fifty-fifty basis with uplifting, concrete and abstractive ideas provided by the staff and attempts by the children to copy the staff items or make their own drawings even if they are piglets, ducks, half moons or something unrecognizable. Sharing half the window or the wall provides the instructor with an opportunity to *lead into* conversation or chatter about the child's drawings, and then move up to the more formalized objects. The instructor chooses words that also introduce the high to low or low to high form of verbal stimulation so necessary to building intellect and then hopefully finding ways to encourage responses.

In a typical instance, an instructor may be returning from an outside activity for training residents and just before she opens the door, she pauses to carry on what amounts to a one-way conversation as the child cannot talk. She points to the lower side of a windowpane where there is an almost recognizable crayon painting of a horse that the child made. She says, "See your horse," "It's a nice horse," "You made that horse," "A horse is good to ride on," or "A horse can ride in a parade." Above the horse is the very real staff photo of the American Flag. So the instructor continues, "In a parade, the horse can carry our flag," "The horse could carry a man and a flag," "That flag is your flag too" or "It means freedom and you can live in a free country."

It will be noted that the chatter contains many different ideas from real to abstract. It really doesn't matter what is said so long as some goal oriented sensible chatter leads to connecting low and high ideas for the child. After many repetitions of moments like this, we observe that the child has learned something because he can accurately point to the flag upon proper stimulation and acknowledge the word *parade*, by pointing to the horse or flag.

This is the process of culturization which is necessary to motivate first and to somewhat lesser extent, second level preaverage intelligence individuals. Preaverage intelligence people especially at the first level of intelligence do not exhibit the spontaneous natural curiosity of the normal children. Preaverage level children do not ask "What made the moon?" "Are the stars lit by candles?" "Who makes the rain?" etc. Normal children thus exhibit their own internal motivation for learning. For preaverage intelligence individuals motivation must be engendered by other people from the outside of their minds by the appropriate kind of stimulation.

Total stimulation includes attempts at learning to read and use numbers, abstractions so important to successful living. There are many methods of doing these but they must be prescriptively and individually programmed for the different levels of preaverage intelligence. A description of any one method would mislead since it might show promise for a girl of emerging societal intelligence but not for a boy at the same level.

Total stimulation or ABC technique also includes structured free play indoors and outdoors. Many games are especially designed to generate behavioral activity of a remedial nature for the child. As always many devices are improvised or invented to promote acceptable behavioral change and learning at the same time.

For example an autistic child (inwardly stimulated) may be introduced on the playground by his instructor to a specially prepared bowling game where the total score is unimportant as is the nature of the competition. Instead the object is to gain reward by small accomplishments leading to larger ones as development occurs. The pins all of the same size have been painted in the four primary colors. Thus one pin is all blue, two are all yellow, three are all green and four are all red. The instructor is taught how to encourage small successes in order to gain larger ones.

A white ball of appropriate size is used. A distance for a successful hit is carefully chosen and this time for a nine-year-old emerging societal intelligence individual, it is two red pins placed side by side at five feet away so that ball can knock both down. After success at hitting, the instructor says, "See you knocked down two red pins" and "We'll put them up again." This time for variation and intricacy, three pins in triangular form are set up five feet away. There is a blue one in front and two red behind it. The ball is thrown and down goes one blue and one red. "Good" says the instructor, "You hit one blue and one red, now let's put them up again."

As days go on the number and variations of pin setting (up to 10) are changed depending upon previous successes. It is obvious that here is a method with a one variable concept (color) to teach both numbers and colors. Actually two variables are present and can be manipulated as necessary. The primary variable is color but the secondary one is number. The variable of distance is controlled for success.

As in any activity in ABC, success is preferably verbally praised (or materially rewarded) for positive reinforcement and neutralized for failure. To be more explicit it is the object of the program to stay as much as possible (75% to 90%) on the positive reinforcement side and minimize punishing, negative or aversive techniques as much as possible. A failure is neutralized when very little is made of it. The instructor's voice is neither raised, nor lowered but she goes casually to another phase. "Let's try this now," not "You didn't do it right" or "That's wrong." The child through positive reinforcement eventually discovers what is right or proper and develops more poise and assurance in performing activities. Aversive technique such as exclusion from desired activity is a last resort in a highly resistive instance.

The play activities indoor and out contain aggression releasors, social activators and relaxation devices.

Total stimulation technique works best when provided in an institution type setting by contact with selectively trained personnel working as a team in a structured setting. The institution might be defined as broadly as a home, a group living setting or a school. Day care systems work partially well. However, the main ingredients are an institution that provides a residential setting and permanently trained personnel.

A residential setting and permanently trained personnel make ABC technique optimally effectively because it allows a variety of helpful circumstances to focus upon the development of a human being at the same time and in the same place. The typical school or institution or service applied for only a few hours is a reasonable compromise but cannot provide the same wholistic developmental convergence of forces. A residential setting has all of these requirements and many advantages.

ABC as an operation is simple yet complex. One cannot see it work in five minutes or half a day because it is too difficult to assimilate the interplay of human exchange that pervades the atmosphere at all times and the background of programming that makes it happen. ABC to the casual observer does not readily flash an answer to an agonizing human problem (that of helping preaverage or retarded to move up the ladder of living) but represents the coordinated knowledge of many learned, experienced, and qualified people working together in a closely knit and well supervised team. In fact, the program would not be possible to operate without spending countless hours daily in team consultation. This is where continuous daily analysis of the affected childrens' diagnoses, problems, progress, programming and procedures are fortified, carefully communicated in understandable language and gradually committed to workable operative form.

A warm interpersonal relationship must be created between residents and staff, so that an atmosphere of love and friendship may evolve at the appropriate and optimal time. The staff, regardless of educational level, must have a lateral relationship to one another and not vertical, so that instructional feedback meetings may provide invaluable bits of knowledge to be applied as skillfully as possible. Close attention to children in small groups including individual treatment where possible, at least some part of every day to make a child feel important and to reinforce special knowledge to allow the brain to attend and absorb.

Finally the creation on a residence of a friendly non-emotionally charged condition wherein a *people to people* atmosphere pervades the situation and mitigates against a too rigid and critical professional view. Included in this phase is a reverence for something spiritual, no matter how simple, to transcend the message that things unseen and unheard may also help the lives of the preaverage.

*Chapter VIII*

# (A)CCEPTABLE (B)EHAVIOR (C)HANGING ABC TECHNIQUES DESENSITIZATION AND NON-NEED FULFILLMENT STIMULATION

P<small>REAVERAGE INTELLIGENCE CHILDREN</small> exhibit many characteristics of behavior that inhibit their mental growth, create behavioral difficulty for themselves, annoy others and in general make it difficult for them to adjust pleasantly and effectively to our society. It is only humane to desire to help them correct these adverse behaviors. In fact, it is imperative if the previously described learning techniques may take hold and allow intelligence to emerge.

In addition, it is necessary to change misbehavior in preaverage or retarded children if relief from a psychological disease known as *twenty-four-houritis* or the problem of incessant demand for attention is to occur. This condition with its daily, weekly, and monthly never ending supervision is a continual problem for people responsible for the welfare of preaverage intelligence children. The inescapability from this burdensome task happens to parents in the home and to personnel in an institution. Without some respite, this disease finally drives these people who care for the children into nervous states which become intolerable. These well-meaning individuals are forced reluctantly, sometimes with guilt feelings, to give up on these preaverage (retarded) children. Sharing the twenty-four-hour burden seems to be the best answer.

In recent years, psychology has given the name *behavior modification* to methods of changing undesirable or unacceptable behavior in certain types of individuals especially those who have been placed in an institution such as one for the mentally re-

## ABC Techniques

tarded. Inherent in the use of the term behavior modification is the obvious fact that all behavior is modified whether good or bad. The term is intended to apply only to misbehavior as perceived by certain individuals who believe there ought to be changes for the more efficient functioning of these affected persons in life and society as well as the institutions.

ABC might be considered a modification of behavior modification in the sense that it more explicitly deals with the changing of certain habits of behavior that are detrimental or ineffective for preaverage intelligence individuals, especially those in the first level preaverage intelligence range (10 to 55). Since behavior modification is a learning technique, the term ABC therefore has a double connotation. It includes the learning methods already described and the changing of undesirable behavior into a more acceptable form. Complete, reformed changes are therefore not always possible or required but some change to a more acceptable degree is implied.

Many of these forms of undesirable behavior may be listed as a starting point for discussion. These are taken from a check list used in the ABC system to perform initial and subsequent systematized evaluations. The following types of misbehavior require instant and constant attention and must be reasonably cleared before learning can effectively take place, although simultaneous change with learning is more the rule than the exception.

1. Aggressive (hits; bites; fights, etc.)
2. Destructive (breaks property, toys, etc.)
3. Self-destructive (bangs head; bites self, etc.)
4. Temper tantrums.
5. Steals (food; property, etc.)
6. Tells lies.
7. Withdrawn (stays alone; hides; doesn't mix, etc.)
8. Fearful to a disturbing degree.
9. Constantly repeats jerky, shaky, rocking or nervous mannerisms.
10. A phobia that distracts attention.
11. Cries or yells constantly.

12. Resistant; Rebellious; Stubborn behavior.
13. Restless; Uncontrollable; Demands constant attention.
14. Constant dependent condition.
15. Engages in unusual sex play with self or others.
16. Lives in a dream world.
17. Displays excessive shyness; hiding; timidity or non-relating loneliness.
18. Misjudges a harmless object for something dangerous.
19. Seems to feel that someone or something is out to *get* him.
20. Responds to voices and/or visions that are not real.

These behavior problems may be common to many children and adults, not just preaverage. However, they must be seen as a matter of degree. Some living in a dream world for short periods (five or ten minutes, even an hour a day) may remain within the bounds of acceptability and be tolerated. However, two hour consecutive periods of misbehavior prevent learning and there is a need for Acceptable Behavior Change to intervene.

In working with first level preaverage, these aberrant behavior patterns become a very difficult thing to ameliorate since most talking and reasoning about them is out of the question. This is why such methods of behavior modification using various forms of conditioning and deconditioning methods were developed.

It is not possible here to describe effective behavior changing techniques for all of the aforementioned list, which is really only partial.

The methods presented are examples of individual prescriptive programming derived from previous experience and successful application. The illustrations closely resemble those used but are primarily teaching devices disguised so as to prevent identification and protect the anonymity of particular persons. The case histories are composites of significant behavior deviations found in many different individuals blended into one illustration so as to indicate the most important teaching principles. In reality these people do not exist as certain identifiable individuals.

Lying and stealing may be amenable to correction by employing the token reward principle which attempts to prolong certain

## ABC Techniques

periods of good or desired behavior. Usually with first level pre-average, an immediate reward given as soon after an event occurs has a more motivating effect. So does a negative or aversive technique. In daily life, an aversive means would usually be employed to correct lying or stealing in the form of verbal scolding or corporal punishment. But ABC theory tries to emphasize the positive approach believing that it produces more permanent results and that it is also more pleasant for first line or contact personnel to administer.

No harsh punishments are used in ABC. The only aversive (negative correction) technique is removal from certain well-liked activities like going swimming (used in the average home) or immediate exclusion for short carefully supervised and measured periods in a place out of sight of others or into a pleasant room. A non-injurious although comfortable chair with gentle and minimum withholding apparatus may occasionally be needed where excessive aggressiveness or tantrum could be dangerous to anybody's life including the child himself. This is referred to as *time outing* and is used in hockey, homes and baseball. Medical supervision is employed for tranquilization or the use of close restraint and this is not the authority of ABC.

Here is an example of a nine-year-old first level preaverage intelligence boy who steals toys, foods or whatever he can get his hands on several times a day. Correction is in order for the sake of his peers who object, the annoyance to the involved personnel and the moral value it would have for the child himself. He like so many understands but doesn't talk. The instructor tells him in terms he can understand what is his and what belongs to others. He shows him or illustrates to be sure he knows the difference. The instructor obtains a plastic bottle into which some visible chips like coins can be maintained.

Team programming helps the instructor first determine what the child likes, such as television, movies, swimming or a bottle of soda at the canteen. Then he takes one of the little red chips and shows the child that if he goes for a certain period of time without taking something preferably for a day, he will get a token he can see in the bottle. The instructor is taught to stretch the good behavior time for five tokens or five days, at which time, the child can go to the canteen for his well-earned bottle of soda. Wrong behaviors get no token or may even lose one. The *good behavior stretch time* is continued and lengthened and gradually includes rewards for other sought after activities and finally settles in successful cases for verbal praise or joyous approval.

This same technique may be used in curbing aggressiveness, tantrums, jerking, rocking, destructiveness or many bad habits.

## Desensitization of Fears or Phobias

Again simultaneously with brain stimulation, procedures may be combined to remove fears or phobias that inhibit learning, distract attention or in general absorb developmental time. Among first level preaverage, fears and phobias abound in all kinds and in all degrees. It should be said, however, that phobias are present in many normal people and cause no problem as long as the stimulus that provokes them is avoided. (I personally would avoid the spectacular view of Paris from the top of the Eiffel Tower. The post card version is very comfortable to me). While many people have this way of easing a phobia, first level preaverage do not.

A girl of first level preaverage intelligence at the self-care acquisitional intelligence range (30 to 44 if you need a score), age 8, exhibited a phobia of water reaching panic-stricken proportions at times. She would not even touch it and would back away in great fright from even the sound of running water from the faucet. Obviously water is a prime necessity to life in drinking, bathing, and, of course, the ever pressing need of toilet training.

Strangely, as is the case with so many preaverage children, they are full of contradictions. Thus she would drink water and liquids of any kind and even seemed to relish them. But bathing was an inhuman struggle, fraught with tears and fighting and toilet training appeared impossible.

Instructional feedback meetings eventually revealed certain characteristics about her behavior. She was more likely to panic when pressed by an adult instructor than by a peer, another child who might be playing with water. At least, she appeared to be able to watch this, and although not tempted to touch the water, she would not erupt into crying. It was also noted that she was very fond of playing with certain toys.

So a program for desensitizing this fear was instituted and communicated in detail so that all of the staff could work in unison. We have found that these programs must have a steady gradual approach. Each small change in procedure seems to work optimally when introduced at one or two week intervals. This means that it can take six to eight weeks to break a phobia, if not to the point of eradication (and this has been achieved in some cases) then to a degree of change that is at least acceptable. This is one reason for calling this system, Acceptable Behavior Change since this permits variations and limitations to change that are tolerable and not substantially interfering with overall effective behavior.

So the first week it was decided to take advantage of the child's milder reaction to watching another child in some phase of water activity. The instructor arranged to have a slightly older child with proper training and instruction to be casually cleaning a wash cloth in a basin. Our phobic resident was quietly introduced to watching this activity from a reasonable distance. The instructor was taught how to give reassuring chatter about the usefulness of the activity and how it didn't seem to hurt the girl doing it. This was performed once or twice a day for brief periods.

It has been found that with preaverage individuals in ABC technique, an exposure to a feared object should not exceed two short periods a day for more lasting results. There is a temptation to go directly to the end result as quickly as possible but this only serves to reinforce and strengthen the fear making it more difficult to change.

After two or three days of observing wash cloth sessions the child was introduced to an observation of a small rubber teddy bear (a previously known favored object) getting a bath in the same basin.

In the second week, the instructor took over some of the washing standing alongside and in a cooperative effort with the slightly older resident girl who was still helping. At the end of this week it was possible for the instructor to take over these duties by herself and the child continued to observe rather quietly.

In the third week, the plan was to introduce an intercessionary or intervening device. For this particular child, there were three such objects, a one-step stool so as to stand on it and observe more closely, a wash brush of particularly attractive coloring, and a larger and most favorite teddy bear made of rubber. An intercessionary device may sometimes work in reducing a phobia because it distracts or accompanies the feared object with a diversionary aspect. This provides interest and a nonprimary focus for a preaverage intelligence child. It seems to be true from observation that preaverage intelligence children can only attend to one thing at a time, if they attend at all, and do not, like the normal child or person, exhibit a peripheral attention to several things.

Since the goal of the procedure, at least in the immediate stages is a nonfrightened girl who can be more easily bathed and toilet trained, with swimming as a latent purpose, the intercessionary devices pave the way or *lead into* the next stage.

For example in the fourth week, the instructor invites the child to stand up on the stool to look more directly into the basin and gradually to extend a helping hand in washing her favorite rubber teddy bear which according to plan is placed face upward in the bowl. The child either timidly puts her hand into the water, or she is helped to do so by the instructor. She is first introduced to the colorful wash brush which she may hold for a while and then, perhaps extend into the water to help wash a leg of her teddy bear. The brush is gradually eliminated in subsequent sessions by allowing her hand to reach further down the handle until it touches the water. All the while she is reassured by encouraging talk to do the best she can and if no fright occurs, further steps may continue.

If at any point in the desensitizing procedure, the fear reaction recurs or intensifies in the child, the process should be interrupted using a neutral means, at least, not turning it into a major event, so that additional fear reinforcement occurs. The interruption should go on for at least a week or two or longer, so that there is a reasonable time for mental erasure to occur. Then the program may be resumed from the beginning if necessary, but more effectively, from a point a little prior to the interruptive incident. ABC experience has established this point in a number of cases.

Programming with feedback meetings continues and in the fifth week, it was decided to move the step stool over to the bathtub, where the most favored teddy bear is placed, this time, purposely, face downward in a small amount of water, maybe an inch or two in depth. Alongside of the animal is the familiar brush and wash cloth. The child is undressed except for diapers or panties for this event for which elaborate procedures have been made. At the appropriate moment, the clothing will be removed and she may begin bathing. At first, however, she is led up the step stool to look and is told or shown that the bear needs to be washed but must not be allowed to keep his face down in the water.

The object is to get the girl to want to go into the tub and turn him around for washing which cannot be done except by being in the tub. If the child will not enter the tub gently with one foot at a time, she may be enticed to do so by the instructor who is also appropriately dressed to stand up in the tub with her. In this type treatment, supporting or instructive personnel must be prepared to meet any type emergency.

So the instructor proceeds into the tub and gradually coaxes the little girl into coming in with her, lured on by the familiar wash cloth, washing brush, and of course, the teddy bear. This step may involve more than a week of gradual attempts at foot wetting, as the teddy bear is rescued and set up straight.

From this point on, the child takes gradual steps toward washing her own feet, and then her own body as she learns to undress completely and gently covers part of herself with lukewarm comforting water. In this phase she can be taught to wash the teddy bear all over so that she gets the mental picture of bathing something entirely. From this stage, the instructor carefully leads the child to wash herself completely. From this base of performance, gradations can be planned for other activities involving water.

Once a breakthrough is made several different procedures involving rewards may be used to extend or transfer the ideas gained. Regression may be expected to set in but generally a little programming and the proper reinforcement should suffice to return movement toward the desired goal. Even if a fear is not completely eradicated but creates less turmoil, can be tolerated, and does not inhibit learning, a behavior change to an acceptable degree has taken place and time for more mental progress has been released.

This process was presented in detail to reveal how fragile and delicate it is to change behavior that is stereotyped and rigid. The degree method with excellent and close front line execution and appropriate intercessionary devices at plateau intervals or times of no progress seems to work best with first level preaverage intelligence individuals.

Beginning intelligence and self-care intelligence preaverage individuals may develop many peculiar and unusual fears that are difficult to change unless careful observation of behavior is made at optimum intervals by knowledgeable personnel. A case in point is that of a ten-year-old boy who seemed to be the only one who did not enjoy riding a hobby horse that was raised slightly on a pole so that it gave a rocking and bouncing effect when properly used. This child also would cry and panic when placed upon it and would eventually never go near it. In its presence in the playground, he withdrew from all activities.

Repeated observations of his behavior and feedback discussions about this hobby horse situation led to a clue that he would panic when the horse was seen from the front. He would not approach from the side or rear either but his reaction was at least a little milder and not as disquieting.

A study of the head of the horse made out of plastic manifested a slightly open mouth with upper teeth protruding just a little. The record did not show that his family owned a horse but the report did indicate the ownership of a large hound dog.

Assuming there was a connection, the psychologist and staff developed a program to dispel the fear. A rather small hound dog with fairly smooth features was introduced by the instructor in play therapy routines on the inside of the residential training unit at certain casual times when other events were also in progress.

For the first week, the instructor introduced this toy dog twice a day in a backward or sideward position, getting the child to pay attention by placing it alongside of our well known cup and shoe. These were familiar objects and the purpose was to entice him to touch and play with this dog to acquire ease with it.

In the second week, a dog with a more pronounced face in which the mouth was slightly open so a tooth or two could be seen was introduced into the process. This animal was larger and stuffed and was made by the staff as so many things have to be in ABC. He was again allowed to play with it in different ways and gradually it was presented to him frontward. He rejected it in this position and had some difficulty enjoying it.

In the third week an intercessionary device, a red coaster wagon which was a favorite of his was introduced outside on the playground and the fairly large stuffed dog was placed in it and he and the instructor took turns pulling the wagon. Even though the dog was placed facing foreward and despite the fact that the child could look back at it, he continued to pull the wagon and seemed to enjoy it.

After a few days of this, a crucial step arrived and the situation outside was set up in preparedness. These are occasions that do not happen spontaneously in ABC method but must be carefully planned. The dog was placed on top of the horse as though riding it backwards. The wagon was positioned on the left side of the horse near the stirrup so that the boy could get up on the wagon, mount the hobby horse properly with left leg in stirrup and right leg over the saddle and hold the dog facing him as he bounced and rocked. The instructor held things in place to make this happen properly.

Eventually the boy was led up to the horse so he could briefly look at the animal from the front. He was then sent around to the side to mount. No fright seemed to occur so the dog was finally removed after a few days and our boy had overcome a fear that seemed very unusual at first. The use of intercessionary devices is again clearly demonstrated in ABC technique.

Desentization by methods like this seem long and extended, and even appear strange but they do leave the child more humanized and wholistic, at least when they work. They don't always do so but when they fail, there is the reasonable outcome that the child is no worse than he was and this cannot be said for some psychological techniques.

### Application of Non-Need Fulfillment Stimulation

This hypothesis suggests that a habit or action may occur when a psychological or physical need of the mind or body requires fulfillment and is therefore self-reinforcing when satisfaction occurs. Hunger, smoking and sex are prime examples. The fulfillment satisfactions attached to nervous tensions such as nail biting or counting fence posts may not be so easily admissible. Yet hundreds of habits attached to inner needs may be more readily apparent.

By a reverse reasoning, if fulfillment happens when the need is not strong or present, the action or habit may be rejected. For want of a better description, this reaction may be called *non-need fulfillment stimulation* and may be used as a corrective or acceptable behavior changing device, especially for habits that are working to the detriment of the individual.

A ten-year-old first level preaverage intelligence boy cannot resist stealing toys and this disrupts the group, prevents others from learning and is not a good moral value. Many direct scoldings serve only to reinforce the attention getting satisfaction derived from this act.

Our ten-year-old is programmed to be given a toy deliberately without any special attention or reinforcement at very fixed and carefully spaced intervals throughout an eight-hour day. For purposes of illustration, we will say that he is presented with the toy every hour on the hour from eight in the morning until five in the evening. The toys are mostly similar but changed occasionally to vary interest level. The theory is that hopefully at some of the times he will not have developed any great inner felt need to steal a toy. This is continued for a while. In several days, if the first sign of rejection occurs, a breakthrough in the habit is possible.

This type of habit interference must be carefully and judiciously applied. When orderly programmed after the first rejec-

## ABC Techniques

tion, the method promises some degree of acceptable behavior change.

It can be used with aggression; fighting, for example, by permitting unreinforced hitting of harmless objects at fixed intervals.

In acceptable behavior changing, not all preaverage intelligence individuals respond. Some can be failures with renewed programming necessary, possibly without too hopeful an outlook.

Some general observations are that contact personnel must be trained not to yell or scold but to remain neutral under trying circumstances of head banging, biting, hitting and destructive behavior. Any form of strong, or even mild disapproval only serves to reinforce and the misbehavior repeats itself.

Acceptable behavior changing requires exacting discipline among personnel over one's personal impulses to lose control. A desire to work painstakingly for an almost imperceptible movement for change is necessary if one is to see the total end result emerge from little bits fitted together. All personnel involved must be satisfied with untold minutes of rewarding happiness in exchange for countless hours of anguish and suffering.

*Chapter IX*

## THE JUDGMENT CALL

EVERY PERSON AT SOME TIME in his life is faced with making decisions for which there are no absolute rules, perhaps no relative rules, perhaps not even precedent. The result is, the individual stands alone, charged with the heavy, even frightening, responsibility to decide by himself the best course of action for himself, and at times even more burdensome, the welfare of others. Sports brings it out very clearly where an umpire or referee, even though trained in his duties and knowing every rule of the game, must face moments when a call he makes depends entirely upon his own judgment.

"He's out," "He's safe" yell two opposing sets of fans at a baseball game. They both believe they're right. However, in the judgment of the umpire he was not—and thousands of dollars go with that decision. It's a *judgment call* because it was a split second mental evaluation of a close play and it took courage and responsibility to make it.

The referee at a football game calls a winning touchdown when the back with the ball sails over the line toward the goal and then is pushed back. In the judgment of the referee, he had gone over the goal long enough and just enough to call the touchdown. The result rests upon a judgment call and someone had to make it.

Life is full of judgment calls for everyone everyday. But too frequently their effects are little realized because the situation is not structured like games are with a set of guidelines and rules. Auto driving is an example. The red light signals a stop and it's easy. But what of the little child who is up ahead with part of his body protruding just a little onto the road from his driveway. Is a stop in order to see what he will do? The decision and responsibility are up to one person—the driver—for there is no red light or even a stop sign.

The judgment call is the daily fare of professionals and other people who work in a helping relationship. A doctor's day is full of these judgments. So is that of a lawyer, clinical psychologist, social worker, personnel manager, nurse, ward aide and in-residence instructors, as I'm suggesting we call them. For you see, many things I've already suggested in this book, even the name *preaverage* is really a judgment call.

Let us step back a moment in history and see how the judgment call got some people to be described as retarded in the first place. It really all began by a comparison of people operating in large settings like a school or industry or living in the complexity of cities as life swirled to intricacies of the machine and its necessity for organization. Certain people had difficulty adjusting to this picture so they seemed *held back* or retarded from maintaining a pace with it. So at a certain point society deemed it humane (a collective judgment call for there are that kind too) to separate these *slow goers* and shelter them out of the way. Those who couldn't find their way to society's sanctuaries were kept at home because of no room in the institution or for fear of society's condemnation to exposure.

Gradually in the last twenty years another judgment has come along; that some of these preaverage are salvageable and useful and ought to be back in a society which at one time said they were too slow to move with it. The collective and individual judgment call now is—Can they make it out there? What can we do to help them? If not, what is best to do for them? These are all judgments which try the souls of certain of the average and above average people who must make the decisions and take the responsibility for them. For you see, the judgment call with pure needs for abstractability is not easily within the province of the preaverage intelligence people.

## This Thing Called Abstraction

To many people abstractive power is a mental ability akin to intelligence and always intangible. Say "calculus" and the engineering professor loves it but the tailor may wonder if it's animal, vegetable or mineral. A preaverage intelligence individual couldn't even dream about it although that big bridge he crosses everyday couldn't have been built without using it. The trouble with abstraction is that it's associated with intellectuals. But it really has shades of meaning and can reach very far down in value.

Reading and numbers are symbols or abstractions and for our first level preaverage intelligence they are extremely difficult to comprehend. *Apple* is something very real, very easy to see and eat—but not so easy to read. *Open* is something one does, not so likely to be seen, certainly hard to eat but easier to read. *Bigger* is a first low level common abstraction and must be mastered before all types of judgment calls can be made.

If a 14-year-old boy of second level preaverage intelligence is asked, "What is money?" he may reply, "It is something you pay debts with, something you can buy things with and spend." A first level preaverage intelligence boy of 14 years might say "Money is quarters, nickels, dimes and pennies." It is observed in comparing the two answers that the boy with a little more intelligence (although still called moderately to mildly retarded today) is revealing some abstraction in his reply indicating an understanding of the word *debt* or a proper use of the function of money. The second boy replies nonabstractively and his concrete answer only tells what some money looks like.

Second level intelligence may understand partially the concept of insurance. However it is still difficult for them to make the judgment that it can be important to life itself in the form of annuity, accident and health or providing disability income. First level intelligence has a most difficult time understanding anything about insurance at all except that it may help someone to pay a bill for a car accident.

The abstractions of the first level preaverage intelligence individual amount basically to some acquaintance with numbers, some reading ability and some communication with words that have an abstractive potential. His learning that in order to buy something, one must pay, and not just take it, borders on abstractive ability. However this is enough of a beginning to direct first level intelligence individuals toward the use of the judgment call so that some form of life in society is possible. The daily living problems or the *off the job problems* may be helped in this way.

## Intelligence and the Judgment Call

In working with human beings with all types of personalities, varying ages and differing mental abilities, such as one finds in a mental hospital or in a residential center for preaverage intelligence people, the number of judgment calls that have to be made daily are countless in number and impossible to evaluate in level of difficulty. In addition these decisions are influenced by varying degrees of education, intellect and intelligence.

In general there is a positive correlation between the degree of intelligence and the relative difficulty level of the judgment call. In other words higher intelligence should be expected to make a judgment call more quickly and in greater complexity. In actual practice this rule does not always follow because emotional states primarily preclude the ability to think with the clarity necessary to make the good or correct judgments on all occasions. It is therefore logical to assume that a difficult judgment call is not easily made by people of preaverage intelligence since here we have in addition to the lower power of intelligence, the same human emotions, feelings and other illness factors complicating the situation. At all levels the desire to make the judgment call is affected by the willingness of the individual to accept responsibility for it.

At the level of beginning intelligence (profound retardation) the judgment call of any kind is practically nonexistent. It is this condition that led to the use of very simplified choice discrimination objects in selected sequential series because this distinction contains a demonstrable element of judgmental exercise. This characteristic of the inability to make a judgment when necessary makes even toilet training difficult at this level. This occurs because certain conditions of personal comfort require the use of effective judgment at a specific time. If the child at the beginning and self-care levels of intelligence takes initiative in going to the toilet at the optimum time or dressing in the proper way as a result of self-stimulation, it can be assumed that humanization is taking place and some degree of judgment call is developing.

The judgment call is the distinct feature of civilization because appropriate decision making represents the highest level of mental functioning that is conducive to good living. As we proceed up the scale into the emerging societal intelligence level we begin to see the judgment call used a little more frequently and effectively. In fact it is this observation that inspired the name societal instead of social because the former implies both living with people and meeting employment or economic conditions whereas social only includes interpersonal relationships.

To become a person of potentially self-sufficient intelligence, an individual must be able to make certain judgment calls that border on the intangible or abstract and determine the difference between successful living in society and possible failure. At this level the idea for example of paying off a debt or indeed even incurring the debt in the first place is a decision in living of first magnitude. Research has shown that at this level some individuals are able to make the judgment call about whether to pay by check or use cash. The approaching average level of intelligence can more easily determine the advantages toward buying or renting a home and some of the responsibilities inherent in work and marriage.

The fact that a person may do work is not always a good indicator of how well a person can live in our society. Many pre-average intelligence people can be trained to work and can perform well for the eight hours required by the job. It is the sixteen hours left after the job, or the *off the job periods* that present the problems to them. The single biggest factor in the occurrence of the *off the job* problem is the inability to make that crucial judgment call.

On an in-residential learning situation for preaverage intelligence individuals such as ABC, the judgment call emerges for all personnel at every level of responsibility. A program to be effective must be executed in great detail by the front line personnel who are always stationed on the premises and therefore in continual contact with the individuals being treated. The closer to a situation the director, supervisor or innovator can be, the better chance there is that responsible judgment calls will effectively be made when spontaneous situations arise. When the distance between the on-premise people and the director, or what can be called the degree of remote control increases, the possibility of error is greater.

Front line personnel in an Acceptable Behavior Change system must be taught to react with poise and calm to the many upsetting and irritating bits of behavior that appear unexpectedly especially in working with first level preaverage intelligence individuals. In the ABC system there are no fixed or regular times for learning because the guidelines try to create a milieu that makes the child most receptive to learning or changing behavior at the optimum moment of alertness and good feeling. The instructor must continually make a judgment call on whether a choice discrimination session will be more effective at 9:00, 10:00, or 10:30 in the morning or 2:00 in the afternoon and everyday this can be different. This is where the in-residence program with its almost home-like atmosphere differs from the usual day school where some rigidity of routines are necessary.

Another crucial judgment call made on the spur of the moment can be illustrated in question form. An instructor working with a very hyperactive child might ask herself, "Should I move up to step $D$ and risk a little frustration, or is it time to back up to step $B$ to give B. I. a feeling of success and then up to $D$ at a more opportune time?" Or how many hugs a day promote love and warmth and are rewardingly used, or are they too often and only add to the dependency problem and become automatic and not growth producing? The professional believes the hugs should be used judiciously.

It's hard to explain this to a mother who ethically and morally believes "Of course it is so right and so easy to hug and just how could it be harmful," that she thinks this professional person doesn't know what he is talking about. The expert agonizes inwardly when indeed the mother is joined by the judgment calls of his own workers. For *hugging* has an emotional overtone that is so appealing while the professional must justify the unattractive reasoning of intellect, and when intellect and emotion encounter each other, the emotion has a way of winning out. However, cooler intellect must grind its way painfully to a more helpful judgment call for this is the essence of professionality. Just ask any surgeon or medical doctor.

Another example of a higher level judgment call made by psychologists and others who use psychological testing, is found not only in the evaluation of test results themselves but in the administration and scoring of these various instruments. It is not at all surprising that the IQ can move up and down when one considers the number of items that appear, especially on individual intelligence tests, that present open-ended or unstructured items for which only so many possibly expected answers can be written into a manual. An occasion arises when a response of this type such as the meaning of a word may almost fit the guide and one examiner scores high while another testor rates the same response low. As the judgment call fluctuates in the mental crucible of even highly trained and knowledgeable people, so does the intelligence level of the child. This result can direct his life into erroneous pathways even though unintended.

### The Application of the Principle or the Law of Parsimony

Parsimony, in the economical, frugal or saving sense, has been used in science and psychology to illustrate a principle or law. Without going into its historical background, this so-called *law of parsimony* may be stated approximately in this manner. It is preferable to explain the truth of an event in as few words as possible rather than try to give an elaborate explanation of the same thing which may be conducive to error. Stated another way the simplest means of approaching a situation to obtain results is to be preferred to some round about long-term action.

Psychiatry, psychology, books and movies have inadvertently made the mysterious, elaborate explanation of behavioral events so fascinating and popular that practically all adults including professionals tend to look for hidden meanings behind what might be simple affairs. Thus an adult may say "She is rejecting me," when in reality the person had no chance to telephone. Or the next door neighbor may be accused of having marital problems and a whole host of reasons built up for this discord all because the husband has been away five times in the last five weeks. The simple explanation is that his mother is very ill and he had to be present to make certain arrangements for her.

One could go on with examples of this type of behavior and the difficulties that can arise from the elaborate explanations when the simple ones might indeed produce some very elemental effective results. People working with preaverage intelligence individuals need to be constantly reminded and appraised of the use of this principle of parsimony.

In self-care instruction one of the exasperating results of toilet training is to have a first level preaverage intelligence child well-trained and then a series of accidents seem to set in. The instructor reports resistive behavior, irritability and general unwillingness to cooperate even to changes in personality. The basic truth is that the child ate a food that can lead to diarrhea. The elemental action that needs to be taken is to call for a standard medical remedy and the situation clears up without even using psychology. People must be reinforced continuously to look for the simple answer first.

A preaverage intelligence child doesn't seem to be able to button his shirt and erupts into a frustrating episode when encouraged to do so. Sometimes everything from regression to mental deterioration is reported for this bit of behavior when the simple explanation is that he cannot make the end of his right index finger meet with the end of his thumb, usually called finger-thumb opposition. His frustrations stop when he is not forced to do what he cannot perform but is unable to tell anyone about it.

One of the most frequent misinterpretations of behavior in children is to report aggressiveness and its attendant frustrations as they are observed in interaction with others. Extensive planning is made to curb the activities of an over aggressive child. The real answer is that in the interacting milieu, he is not the one at fault. Closer observation reveals the plain truth that another boy is pinching him and the first child is responding in a disturbed way. The cure is simple, the pincher is removed and our child becomes his usual serene self.

When misbehavior is discussed or observed in the human individual, the principle of parsimony should be observed and helpers should be trained to look first for the simplest clue that will explain it. When this is not adequate, a series of hypotheses should be tried gradually until elaborate treatment more nearly justifies the remedy.

There is some reason to believe that the principle of parsimony and the judgment call may be closely related; if not brother and sister; then at least first cousins.

## Attempting to Improve the Judgment Call for Preaverage Intelligence Individuals

What can be done to improve the judgment call for preaverage intelligence individuals? In order to shed some light toward seeking a possible answer for this question which is most crucial for preaverage intelligence individuals and their successful community adjustment, we must hypothesize from research and observations that there are some clues worth noting that point in a promising direction.

For purposes of illustration the preaverage intelligence people will again be divided into two groups which we've used so often, the first level preaverage intelligence (called trainable retarded), and the second level preaverage intelligence (called educable retarded).

For the first level preaverage intelligence individuals the skillful application of total stimulation techniques so that abstractiveness can be introduced in relative degrees seems to indicate a method of promise. The progression from choice discrimination through directions and purposive talkativeness provides a basic challenging means for mental development. Introducing the triangle to pyramid sequence may seem at first impossible of mental absorption but one might be surprised when an 18-year-old of emerging societal intelligence uses the pyramidal shape as a means of decoration in a sheltered workshop where the middle of the pyramid has a hole to place a candle.

Moving up to second level preaverage intelligence especially in the teenage and older period where at least simple conversation is a possibility, cognitive-didactic feedback counseling in small groups or in individual sessions may produce results more closely related to the important judgmental decisions. Many individuals at this level respond to counseling that involves abstractive concepts that are stimulating at their own level of thinking and maintain the challenge of trying to learn just a step or so ahead of themselves.

For example, topics like this will frequently draw sensible responses when properly structured and used. A subject such as *The Value of Life* with its related searching into *Good and Evil* or *The Responsibility of Acceptable Conduct*.

A topic such as *What is the Government?* and *Who is the Government?* seems to stimulate the judgment more than a moderator might expect.

Further subjects such as *The Value of Friends* so greatly needed by everybody and so very helpful to the preaverage is a very moving topic. *The Nature of Work and its Value for Life* should be gone into quite thoroughly.

*The Effective Use of Leisure Time* is a most rewarding topic for help especially with the *off the job* problems. For some of these people even taking the subjects of *Learning and Thinking;* including *The Make-up of the Brain and Some of Its Functions* all the way up to the *Nature of the Universe* and back down to earth for the importance of *Marriage and Its Meaning,* have not been found to be beyond some responsible judgments by these preaverage intelligence individuals.

In conclusion, it might be suggested that the people whose intelligence places them in the upper three quarters of mental ability in our society should use their talent to stimulate the one quarter preaverage intelligence individuals into more reasonable effort, accept them in a friendlier and closer relationship, accord them an opportunity to show their capability and finally prepare an environment in which they can flourish better. This combination of factors may provide the best hope that preaverage intelligence individuals can find their place in society and possibly render a contribution to its progress.

# INDEX

**A**

ABC (*see* Acceptable behavior change)
ABC method of directions
  examples of, 37
  instruction of, 36
  instruction, timing of, 36
ABC method of learning and behavior changing, 12-13, 18, 19
  abstraction, instruction of, 45-46
  abstraction, presentation of, 32
  activities of, 42
  color, presentation of, 32-34
  components of, 20
  definition of, 13
  effectiveness, conditions for optimal, 46-47
  environment for, 42
  form, presentation of, 32, 34-35
  foundation, motivational, 20
  game, use of, 45-46
  motivation, objects of, 22
  music, presentation of, 43 (*see also* Stimulation, total)
  objects presented
    selection, reasons for, 22
  objects presented, advancing groups of, 27-31
  objects presented, groups of mixing between, 24
  objects presented, number of reasons for, 23
  objects presented, realistic nature of, 26-27
  objects presented, sample of, 21
  personnel of,
    abilities, judicial, 64-66 (*see also* Judgment call)
  personnel, training of, 64-65
  presentation, horizontal method of, 21
  presentation, left diagonal approach to, 25-26
  presentation, left-sided configuration approach to, 26
  presentation, order of reasons for, 22-23
  presentation, right diagonal approach to, 25-26
  presentation, right-sided configuration approach to, 26
  presentation, variations in approach to, 25-26
  presentation, vertical approach to, 25
  principles involved, 20
  puzzles, use of, 38-41
  reinforcement during, 46
  stories, presentation of, 43
  success of, 13
  techniques of, aversive, 46, 51
  techniques of, motivational, 50-51
  techniques of, total stimulation, 43, 68
    environment for, 46
    personnel for, 46
  techniques of, visual, 43-44
Acceptable behavior changing
  development, reasons for, 16, 50
  technique of, degree, 56
  techniques of, 51-59
Amentia
  terminology, use as, 4

**B**

Barrett, Dr. Albert M., v, vii, 3
Behavior, change of (*see also* Acceptable behavior changing)
  methods, stimulation, 13
  principle, immediate reinforcement, 14
  programs for, 42
  techniques, desensitization, 13
Behavior modification, 13, 17 (*see also* Acceptable behavior changing)

acceptable behavior changing compared with, 49
discussion of, 48-49

## C
Carver, George Washington, 44
Choice discrimination, 36, 38, 42, 63, 65, 68
development of, 35
Commands (*see* Directions)
Culturization, process of, 44-45

## D
DDCC principle, 24
Defectiveness, mental
terminology, use as, 4
Directions (*see also* ABC method of directions)
components of, 36
instruction in, importance of, 37
types of, 36-37
types of, multiple, 37

## E
Emotionality, 9

## F
Feeblemindedness
terminology, use as, 4

## H
High intelligence, low achiever, 11
HILA (*see* High intelligence, low achiever)

## I
Idiot
terminology, use as, 4
Imbecile
terminology, use as, 4
Instructor, in-residence, 17
judgment calls of, 61
Intellect (*see* also Mentation, cognitive)
animals and, 10
definition of, 10
discussion of, 11
environment affecting, 15
intelligence affecting, 10
nature of, 11

Intellect, development of
blocks to, 11 (*See also* High intelligence, low achiever)
Intelligence (*see also* Mentation, cognitive)
animals and, 10
characteristics of, 24 (*see also* DDCC principle)
definition of, 10
definition of, discussion of, 9-10
determination, genetic, 15
discussion of, 11
factors of, inhibitory, 15-16
intellect and, interaction between, 15
measurement, difficulties of, 11, 12
nervous system affecting, 12
stimulation, bi-sensory
value of, 43
stimulation, sensory, 16, 17-18, 19, 23, 43 (*see also* Stimulation, total)
stimulation, verbal, 23, 43, 44
Intelligence, approaching-average, 7, 13
Intelligence, beginning, 7, 13
judgment call and, 63
Intelligence, emergence of
atmosphere for, 20
encouragement of, 16-17
program for, 17-19, 22-29 (*see also* ABC method of learning and behavior changing)
Intelligence, emerging societal, 7, 13
Intelligence, first level preaverage, 19
characteristics of, 16
definition of, 13
Intelligence, increase of
research in, 15
Intelligence, level of
judgment call and, relationship between, 63-64
Intelligence, potentially self-sufficient, 7, 13
Intelligence, preaverage (*see* Preaverage intelligence)
Intelligence, second level preaverage, 19
definition of, 13
Intelligence, self-care acquisitional, 7, 13
Intelligence quotient, 4

# Index

alternatives to, 4
classification system, Barrett
  effects of, positive, 7-8
  intelligence and, differences between, 15
  interpretation of, alternative, 5
  interpretation of, lateral, 5-6
  interpretation of, vertical, 4-5
  effects of, 6-7
  variations in, 15
  variations in, reasons for, 66
Intelligence testing (*see* Testing, intelligence)
Intelligence values
  effect of, interactive (table), 5
  persons below average, number of, 5
  position of, people in lateral (table), 6
I.Q. (see Intelligence quotient)

## J

JND (*see* Just noticeable difference)
Judgment call (*see also* Intelligence, level of)
  definition of, 60
  discussion of, 60-61
  emotion affecting, 63
Just noticeable difference, 39
  discussion of, 19

## L

"Law of Parsimony" (*see* Parsimony, law of)
"Lead into familiarity," 24
Learning
  attention affecting, 36
  methods of, 15
Learning, graduated method of, 19
Learning, measurement of
  factors affecting, evaluation of, 19
Learning, methods of (*see* ABC method of learning)
  principles, immediate reinforcement, 14
Lincoln, Abraham, 44

## M

Memory, 9
Mentation, cognitive
  definition of, 9
  expression of, formula, 12
  processes of, 10
Moron
  terminology, use as, 4

## N

Nervous system
  nature of, electrochemical, 11

## O

Ohm's Law, 11, 12

## P

"Parsimony, law of"
  definition of, 66
  use of, 66-67
Preaverage, 3 (*see also* Retardation, mental)
  connotations of, 3
  terminology, use as, 9
Preaverage intelligence, vii
  classification system, Barrett, (table), 7
  definition of, 16
  measurement of, erroneous, 12
  problem of, basic, 11
  testing of, alternative, 12
Preaverage intelligence individuals
  ability of, work, 64
  abstraction, understanding, 62-63 (*see also* ABC method of learning and behavior changing)
  attention, discussion of, 36
  attention span of, 19-20
  behavior, correction of undesirable, 48
    techniques of, 51-59
  behavior, undesirable, 49-50
  characteristics of, 20, 45
  judgment call and, 61
  judgment call, improvement of, 68
    program for, 68-69
  motivation of, 9, 45 (*see also* Culturization, process of)
  parents of
    abilities, judicial, 65 (*see also* Judgment call)
  phobias, desensitization of, 53-59

phobias, discussion of, 52
stimulation of, verbal
 importance of, 23
President's Commission on Mental Retardation, 3
Psychology
 contributions of, 3
Puzzle, jigsaw (*see also* ABC method of learning and behavior changing
 difficulty, determination of, 39
 gradation of, ABC, 39
 importance, educational, 40-41
 nature, realistic, 38
 value, educational, 38-41

**R**

Retardation, borderline, 6, 13 (*see also* Intelligence, approaching-average)
Retardation, borderline mental
 terminology, use as
 effects of, 6-7
Retardation, educable mental, 4
Retardation, mental, 3 (*see also* Pre-average)
 attitudes, creation of, 3
 connotations of, 3
 definition of, 16
 development of, 3-4
 persons identified, number of, 5
 ratings of, intelligence (table), 6
 semantics of, vii
 terminology, use as
 effects of, 7-8
Retardation, mild, 6, 13 (*see also* Intelligence, potentially self-sufficient)
Retardation, moderate profound, 6, 13 (*see also* Intelligence, emerging societal)

Retardation, profound, 6, 13 (*see also* Intelligence, beginning)
Retardation, severe, 6, 13 (*see also* Intelligence, self-care acquisitional)
Retardation, trainable mental, 4

**S**

Stimulation, non-need fulfillment
 example of, 58-59
Stimulation, total, 68
 components of, 45-46
 definition of, 42
 value of, 43

**T**

Test results, intelligence
 judgment call affecting, 66 (*see also* Intelligence quotient)
Testing, intelligence
 categorization of, 4
 problems of, 11
 use of, 4
 value of, 3
Thinking, beginning of
 definition of, 3
"Time outing," 51 (*see also* ABC method of learning and behavior changing, techniques of, aversive)
Toilet training, 52, 54, 67
 difficulties of, 63
Total stimulation (*see* Stimulation, total)
"Twenty-four-houritis," 48

**W**

Washington, Booker T., 44
Washington, George, 44